ENGAGING WITH REALITY

The personal Christian relevance of everyday experience

J. F. GORDON

Second Edition

1

ISBN 978-0-9570970-5-6

"I will give them singleness of heart and action so that they will always fear me for their own good and the good of their children after them."

Jeremiah 32:39

"Abstraction ... always means impoverishment and depletion so far as direct perception is concerned."

Ernst Cassirer after A G Baumgarten

Contents

Preface

Although I am approaching the subject of this book as a physician, I am aware that the way people generally see doctors in our present culture rather obscures what I would mean by a physician's approach to it. By admitting to having qualifications in medicine I am liable to be seriously misunderstood. Yet the realities to which I refer involve the meaning of personal relationships, the effects of events upon soul and body, and personal suffering. Generally speaking, members of the medical professions, through the very nature of their everyday activities, have more detailed, more disinterested and more extensive knowledge of this sort of thing than most other people. Therefore it must inevitably fall to a physician to write this sort of book, although it is not written from the perspective of medical science, nor is it written from the perspective of scientific psychology. It is in fact the sort of Christian theology that theologians have neglected, because physical medicine has been allowed to take the hegemony and ignore spiritual considerations.

People who suffer in their bodies or in their minds go to the doctor in the belief that in this day and age medical science should be able to fix it. In Britain over the past two hundred years or so, since the Industrial Revolution, governments have perceived a need for medical treatment to be made available through institutions regulated and sanctioned by the state, and people have become accustomed to rely on state provision. The efficient management of distress, mental or physical, in large numbers of people has been necessary in order to keep the peace. Rational secular methods of treatment, and institutions to house and investigate the most troublesome conditions, have been developed to cater for vastly various people with diverse systems of belief. These days in England the General Medical Council, the National Institute for Clinical Excellence and the medical Royal Colleges make sure that doctors treat and prevent illness according to scientific principles. Since the Second World War treatment and advice has been provided by the National Health Service free at the point of access, which is of course a major vote winner. So lay people have commonly come to understand illness only in terms of what members of the secular medical professions do to them.

Consequently, illness and suffering have generally been considered as subjects to be understood mechanistically, and not in any other meaningful way. The body is thought of as a physico-chemical machine that should be mended when necessary with chemicals (drugs) or surgery. And people speak of "my body" as a thing, an object separate from their actual person. And commonly they have great difficulty associating the meaning of their experiences with effects in their bodies.

Sadly, most Christian churches have been powerless to offer a credible Biblical alternative to what is offered by the secular state, although their Lord Jesus Christ plainly healed all who came to him. Their involvement with distress and suffering has largely been confined to comforting prayer, philanthropic good works, and opinions about ethics. Otherwise they have effectively insisted that most human suffering be categorized as illness to be dealt with by the medical profession.

Yet it has always been possible to see beyond the confines of academic disciplines, and to apply God's word to absolutely every aspect of human experience, including every aspect of distress and illness. And new translations of the Bible have made it easier to allow the Holy Spirit to reveal the depths of meaning in the word of God. But few have ever had the courage to think outside the box in God's way. Most Christians still depend for their understanding of themselves upon academic science, philosophy and theology.

Academic disciplines have their place nonetheless. They serve a political function in creating the rationale for the organization of systems and institutions that keep the peace by providing in a secular way for people's immediate needs. They provide a sort of Band-Aid or splint for when we are weak. In this diverse, impersonal and overcrowded world we all need to be able to fall back on secular hospitals and welfare agencies and use what they offer. We can be grateful for them. Discerning people, however, would be wise not to lose sight of the fact that the academic disciplines and politics that control such organizations are secular, not Christian.

Secular professional scientists, philosophers and theologians have usually become so entrenched in their disciplines that they could never tell the Christian gospel in a simple way even if they knew it. Their peers place upon them demands to use arguments and language that are academically acceptable. To break out of the mode would not only be seen as a betrayal of the fraternity to which they have given their allegiance but would also threaten the tenure of their positions and undermine their financial security.

By their very nature academic disciplines are abstract, and therefore only partly relevant to concrete lived reality. And one of the arguments made in this book is that they are abstract because they are academic, sceptically omitting relationship through the Lord Jesus Christ with almighty God, creator of the universe.

As a general physician and a medical psychotherapist in the market place I have been privileged to attend to the narratives of hundreds of people in all sorts of circumstances, whilst focusing my responses on possibilities for actual healing. And whilst I studied all the subjects required for professional accreditation, and kept abreast of new developments, by the grace of God the Spirit of the Lord Jesus Christ encouraged me to keep my mind open to his instruction too. I have therefore, been compellingly challenged to make sense in his way of what I perceived, and not only to make sense of the experiences, reactions and social behavior of other people, but also to make my own experiences and reactions right with God as I listened.

The academic disciplines of medicine, psychology, psychiatry, psychoanalysis, philosophy and theology proved inadequate for me. The only way that made the sort of sense that brings real peace and healing was simply taking God at his word.

This way is available to everyone who accepts the Lord Jesus. It is not dependent upon academic or professional qualifications.

God wants all his people to enlarge the place of their tent (Isaiah 54:2) in this respect so as to understand people and relationships, and healing, his way, according to his word.

Chapter 1 - Experience

Just as everyone learns from their mother, as a child, because they believe in her, so our minds continue to change according to whom we believe. Of course, as we grow older there will be many other people we'll have believed in, and there will be some who will not have been good enough in certain respects. But disappointments can become learning experiences. If we have already known enough love and truth we can learn to discriminate, and to work things out for ourselves accordingly. So our experiences are made sense of through the people we find credible enough. And the path we take when we interpret events and use our reason is influenced by the personal relationships that have given substance to sense.

In this book it is not the author you should entirely believe but rather almighty God. Listen to him as you read it! Although the author has no desire to manipulate people through abstract reasoning, nor to persuade them through psychological techniques into ways of seeing and behaving that may bring glory to anyone else other than to the God of Israel and Jesus Christ his only begotten son, what is written here should be checked against the word of God in Scripture, and anything that is not right with him should be discarded. The author's intention is to be a sort of good mother who enables his revelation in you through telling you about personal experience of reality in this world in relation to the kingdom of heaven. So since it is for the glory of God, let us see clearly by allowing the Spirit of God to be the light to our path, in the hope that the book may be a help in the process of learning from our experiences, including the confusion and knockbacks and pains that beset us from time to time, for Jesus took it all on the cross. If it becomes possible to see more clearly and receive some of God's understanding of what is going on, it will be easier to avoid deception, so that our pilgrimage through this world as members of his kingdom may lead more efficiently to our proper place in eventual union with him.

Every one of us lives under the authority of one spiritual allegiance or another. And belief in a deity is more powerful in the long run than belief in another human being. Since from this spiritual point of view it can be seen that everyone is obedient to a deity of some sort or other whether they are aware of the fact or not, it follows that our minds become conformed in obedience to the one we worship, whether our worship is conscious or whether it is merely subliminal. And as children our minds will first have been formed in obedience to the deity our mother worships, although we shall not be aware of whom that deity may have been until much later.

The God who created mankind in his own image and gave us life is the living God of love who heals; and his pure, healing, living Spirit is accessible through calling on Lord Jesus Christ. It is available by thankfully accepting redemption from the fallen half-dead sinful state through Jesus' blood which was shed to save us. Such is the grace of God that if we recognize and accept what Jesus his son did for us on the cross he redeems us out of our sin, and brings us into his kingdom. He opens our understanding so that we may know something of his mind,[1] and sheds his light so that we perceive truthfully his way, and opens our hearts so that we love with generosity. In the kingdom of heaven there is no sickness, pain, shame or deception; and as we work free of our fallen nature by responding to him with love, by really allowing ourselves to know him and by taking his words seriously, we find healing.

In order to receive this benefit, however, it is necessary for us to act on his word in faith, and to continue to do so. Passivity leaves one fallen. You do what he says. You do not expect him to do it all for you. You engage with him moment by moment as you live in this world. You maintain the relationship in all the vicissitudes of your life. Worship is active.[2] It brings the kingdom of God to you as you step out righteously in relationship with him. Then there is healing for spirit, soul and body. The kingdom of God is applied directly into our activity. It has real personal meaning. It is no

---

[1] 1 Corinthians 2:16.
[2] Romans 12:1, James 1:22, 2:14-26.

longer just some ideal in the mind. We embody resurrection power and inevitably become salt and light in this world.

Faking this is deception. It could even be a killer. Passively going along with a form of religious observance without real engagement could mean that your heart is not really in it. If you are actually calling on a person to be your Master, this is a serious business. In order to meet him personally so as to believe in him, it is necessary to call on the Lord Jesus Christ of Nazareth personally by name. After all, who is worshipped is fundamental, and you cannot afford to invoke the wrong person. There are many deceivers, and from the world of spirits whomsoever you actually or effectively call upon will appear. The only way into the presence of the one true God is through the Lord Jesus Christ his son who was born in Bethlehem, whose mother was Mary, who was raised in Nazareth and who was crucified but rose from the dead.

Satan is alive and active. He is beautifully seductive, too, brilliantly clever, ruthlessly manipulative, subtly deceiving, excitingly degenerate, and deadly. Very seriously he challenges God's authority in every aspect of personal and social life in order to seduce people into his principality of eternal death. Who has sufficient discernment to avoid him?

In this world we people, whether we know it or not, are caught in a spiritual war between God and Satan, and always, in everything that occurs in the life of each one of us, we need to be discerning so as to choose whom to believe. Our actual lives ultimately depend on it.

All the academic and technological brilliance of this world, with its logical abstract reasoning, and its practical solutions for ease and pleasure and provision of what we want, is not ultimately as strong as what may appear to be the foolishness of God. Secularism is under the command of a god who deludes us if he can with a false sense of security, and who hypnotizes people into a sort of stupor as they trust machines to look after them. Although machines are very useful, unthinking reliance on technological convenience may limit the capacity for spiritual awareness and understanding. In this way people fail to realize their need of that extra dimension of adaptability and security that comes from a loving relationship with the living God, who provides the discernment and wisdom necessary to love and be loved freely. Secularists are inclined to work things out in their heads with abstract reasoning and natural ingenuity using the logic and rules they have been taught; although without God their efforts will not be as mature and free as they could be. They will lack the dimension of accord with the will of God, because their hearts are not opened to him, and their perception not attuned to him, and in consequence their understanding will be actually more limited than they know.

The increasing demand upon health services, and popular addiction to the reassurance of scientific medicine, may be seen as signs of this secularism. Both the living body and the mind are commonly treated as objects that need things done to them in order to keep going. People are cut off from themselves. Knowledge of living connection between spirit, mind, soul and body, and of the impossibility of separating these different aspects of the individual person, except as theoretical abstractions, is largely lost. So too is the knowledge of how experience of social relationships may affect the spirit, mind, soul and body. The meaning of what is going on has become a matter of abstract supposition, rather than of intuition and revelation influenced by Holy Spirit and tempered by intelligence so as to become embodied wisdom.

Modernism demands that medical technology should fix every inconvenience of body or mind without really knowing the meaning. The continuous improvements in the quality of life demanded by modernism are technological advances in convenience rather than growth in personal maturity and wisdom.

Postmodernism seems an even more degenerate result of the spiritual complacency engendered by passive dependence upon secular attitudes. There is widespread rejection, in the postmodern culture, of any notion that personal meaning may count in anything but a superficial, ephemeral way. Any suggestion that perceptions and reactions are influenced by traditional Christian values is dismissed. The cultural attitude is that personal influences may take you this way or that, but the way taken is neither here nor there: it has no eternal or profound significance for life or death; it is merely a lifestyle choice that you found yourself making. You may even fall in love, but of course the likelihood is that the person you love will be unfaithful. Why face the pain? Healing is impossible! Even if it mattered nothing really meaningful and substantial could be done about it. The best thing to do is just to take the pills. There is life, there is death, and life seems better than death so long as it feels good. As Solomon said in Ecclesiastes, essentially everything is meaningless. Sensations may produce thrills of one sort or another and you can live for the excitement. You may have visions and supernatural experiences that may lead to creative fantasies and amazing understandings, and you can choose for yourself what it all means and what you do with it provided you create a narrative that seems to justify it. In the postmodern culture nothing has a meaning that should not be doubted. All disinterested intellectual interpretations that include perceivable evidence are reckoned valid. Every choice may be as fascinating as the next. And advances in mathematics, science and technology have enabled extraordinary use to be made of them.

All this scepticism yields no teleological meaning beyond mathematical significance, which nevertheless can gain you advantage in practical endeavours, in earning a living, and in competition with others. The suggestion that it can bring no lasting peace to the soul is dismissed. Consequently there is really no lasting soundness in the emotional space, only confusion, emptiness and ennui. Secularists accept this as inherent in the human condition and even celebrate it as part of the richness of diversity.

Out of the blue, of course, something may occur to render the person hopeless. Some illness, some loss, some assault or overwhelming catastrophe may suddenly be devastating. But if it should then become impossible to feel good any longer there will, of course, be a drug to make you feel better. You may even have to live as some sort of cripple, but if that should be the case the state or some philanthropic charity will help you out. Medical and psychological science can manipulate the way you perceive for your apparent benefit.

Because there are so many answers, so many aids, so many cures, official bodies will support only what academics offer as value for money. Beyond that it is politically incorrect to ask, "What does it all mean?" Faith in a God whose face may be sought for healing seems ridiculous after the devastations caused by so much war. In a society full of diverse beliefs, and in the absence of credibly authoritative Christian apologetics and guidance from the established church, politicians have decided that the only way to keep the peace, and to avoid litigation from offended parties is to enforce secular humanism through an obligation to be politically correct.

So as the postmodern culture has prevailed, paganism in one form or another has been given equal political standing with Christianity. It presumes, furthermore, to take the hegemony by imperiously demanding, "Why did you say that?" The spiritual Christian case is dismissed as invalid, the word of God is rubbished, and law is executed in favour of pagan values.

Those who reach a point in their lives when they are desperate enough to search for real truth, however, and who decide to seek the face of the God of Israel and accept Jesus his son, and those people, too, who are available to help in that quest, would be wise to be careful to seek God's guidance in order to know how to be shrewd as snakes and innocent as doves as Jesus recommends,[3] so as to persevere against the opposition. Safe houses will be needed where it is acceptable to be passionate and to believe with all the heart, because without emotion, and without ascribing meaning to emotion, there is no true soundness in personal relationship, and without truth personal relationships are deceptive, and deception cankers the soul. Shrewdness is particularly necessary because the probability is that most places and people who actually call themselves Christian will be no help at all. Real Christian hospitality will be found only through nous.[4]

It is the god you effectively worship who gives meaning to your experience. The god of humanism will influence you to find his sort of meaning through his humanistic truth if you belong to him, and the God of Israel will influence you to find his meaning through his eternal truth if you seek his face through Jesus. The meaning is conveyed not primarily through intellectual reason but through knowing and giving your heart to your god like a child and following him. It is conveyed spiritually in relationship, just as a mother tells her child about the world the babe is born into.[5] The God of Abraham, Isaac, Israel and Jesus will do this throughout our lives in such a way that each one of us may eventually stand before him and give a truthful account and be not guilty. He will enable us to overcome deception and all accusation through the power of the Holy Spirit living in us, and he will enable us to

---

[3] Matthew 10:16.
[4] Isaiah 11:3.
[5] Mark 10:15.

overcome our fallen human nature so that it will not prevail in this world. This will involve opening our eyes and ears and hearts to perceive truthfully in God's way, which will always accord with holy Scripture. The whole universe holds together and makes sense in him and he will show us as much as we need to know.[6] We find new life, eternal life and healing, as we follow his path with him.

Any perception we make that is not absolutely real and true will fail to give full honour to God. And since each one of us is created in his image, any perception not absolutely real and true may be expected ultimately to affect us unhealthily. The word 'real' applies to things and events, some of which may be misperceived. Events are occurrences in dynamic context involving things and individuals with other contingent things and individuals. Facts are perceived in a context that is always more than we know, for the context is not only physical but also spiritual. They are perceived according to what has been learned and according to prevailing influences. The word 'true' applies to how apparent facts are interpreted. Truth is the person who reveals and interprets perceived data. And the individual who has truly accepted Jesus has the free will and power to be obedient to righteous perception and belief.

What is experienced through the senses is interpreted by each individual person according to who has been believed. Even the secularists, postmodernists and sceptics interpret data and events according to whom they have actually believed. The interpretive influence is

---

[6] Colossians 1:17; 1 Corinthians 2:16.

spiritual, and gives meaning to the individual person which may or may not be shared. Faith is believing in someone and acting on it. This is what gives substance to things hoped for, and evidence to things not seen, and understanding.[7]

Verbal responses are uttered as a result of our experiences according to past understanding. One way or another we speak about what occurs in order to declare our response and effectively check it out with others, which indicates our present position in relation to it and to them. The validity and relevance of our responses become apparent in relation not only to the other people we have believed in but also to the society in which we find ourselves and whose language we share.

Interpreted experience we name perception. It is our perception that determines our subsequent behaviour. When there is no smidgen of doubt about a perception, however, we call it prejudice or foreclosure, and wise people will always be leaving room for the Spirit of God to correct them.[8] Certainty must always be suspect. You can be certain about whom you love but not about your theoretical constructs.[9] But this is not to say that your theoretical constructs will be unproductive. What you cannot be certain of is their ultimate value.

---

[7] Romans 10:17; Hebrews 11:1-3.

[8] 2 Timothy 3:16-17. René Descartes knew this uncertainty and doubt, but did not understand Scripture well enough, despite his Jesuit education. His mistaken search for certainty has misled countless Christians for four centuries. This is discussed further in Chapter 6.

[9] My wife Pamela said this! Psalm 119:96 refers.

Experience

When experience has initiated a formative behavioural response, it is remembered. Our current understanding comes from making sense of what is going on through making sufficient connections between various aspects of present experience and memory of past experience. Thus we make a sufficient totality of the sensations and influences and people who influence us to respond to experiences with some degree of courage. But of course future experiences, and deliberation upon them, may modify memory, perception and understanding.

Scientists have established that there are fairly direct connections in the brain between sensory neurons and motor neurons so that what is experienced via the senses results in motor responses through which meaning is perceived, with contributions from centres in the brain for emotion and centres in the brain for speech. These neurological connections play a part not only in giving meaning to immediate experience but also in the development of understanding and memory.[10] So both the phenomenology and the Scripture are vindicated by the science.

Our inevitable insecurity in the wide world, and the need for negotiation in every aspect of social life amongst other people, naturally begets anxiety about the weakness of our standing and the weakness of our case. And it seems quite possible that this natural social anxiety begets the heightened awareness we call consciousness, through similar neurological systems.

---

[10] M. Fabbri-Destro and G. Rizzolatti: *"Mirror Neurons and Mirror Systems in Monkeys and Humans,"* Physiology vol. 23 no. 3, 171-9, June 2008.

Unless our responses are met in truth, however, it is logically possible that we may eventually lose our way, become confused, perplexed, or even quite stultified. Paranoia may even take over if rejection, fear or bitterness become overwhelming Then our alertness and conscious awareness will become stressed and exceptionally acute. But the firmer our faith, and the more it rests soundly in truth and love, the better our understanding will be, and the stronger our case and the greater our courage and security. But then the greater will be our need carefully to make our case with others because of their natural envy. We shall need to protect ourselves by being clear about where we stand with them. Therefore stress remains.

What comes into consciousness at any particular moment can be taken hold of and deliberated upon with others. The deliberations inevitably take into account thoughts of others, which will influence us. If God is included, through Holy Spirit living within the person, and if thoughts are brought into conformity with the word of God, then his peace comes.[11]

What is experienced does not always make sense, however, and perplexing memories may, quite commonly, cause us periodic distress. If our experience cannot be made sense of adequately, with the help of people we have believed in, it will be troublesome. The resulting gaps in understanding are often anxious, fearful, angry and emotional, and may lead to blocks to maturity. If people in consequence dismiss our partial account as inadequate, or even as invalid, the facts of

---

[11] 2 Corinthians 10:5.

that painful experience of rejection will be laid down in our own memory. If such faulty memory is buried deep in the unconscious, with the intention, for whatever reason, of never bringing it to light, it will nevertheless have a constantly stressful effect upon us. Hidden wounds and emotions exert some effect on our speech and behaviour. Memories buried like this may suddenly become consciously remembered in unforeseen circumstances which seem to indicate their relevance. But they are susceptible to future modification and healing.

There may occasionally appear to be serious gaps in a person's memory, and for some people, all that is remembered on occasion may be horror, anxiety, fear, dread, rage, or other powerful emotion, threatening to energize the whole body dangerously, or stultifying confusion that renders the person unable to relate. It will be found that the full truth of such memory gaps has never come to light; but God knows the whole truth of what was happening then, and he can heal those gaps. There are many people who have been crippled by particular experiences and who have not yet found healing, people with hidden insecurities, or with aspects of themselves that have not yet known the peace of God. This hinders the development of fuller maturity.

Of course, people whom we have believed in the past may have been misguided. We too may have been misguided. Our understanding may have been faulty. We too may have come to false conclusions. Other people may have been wilfully cruel, manipulative and deceptive. There may have been unspeakable shocks and trauma. Past experience as personally perceived is, nevertheless, a determinant of future behaviour.

Therefore people cannot be expected to behave according to other people's expectations just by being instructed to do so. Past experience may often be in need of healing. Therefore when people are punished for offences, healing should be offered too.

Allowances will always need to be made for imperfections in others. Each one of us may be imperfect in all sorts of ways, and each one of us would be wise to make time and space not only for recall and reflection in order to make connection with memories and associations to past events, but also for the disturbances associated with the realizations and changes in perception that may occur. We need individual space that is safe and secure enough for this sort of thing. We need to go into our room and shut the door and talk to God. And we also need folk who can let us be, folk to be understanding enough to contain what is going on without getting too upset, and folk who can keep secrets, who respond wisely in truth, and who will be authentically present in love without domination. So there is a great need for maturity amongst Christians.

Despite all this, the law of the land must uphold the ideal that human beings should be accountable in godly truth, and are responsible for their behaviour, and it is not excessively difficult in a Christian culture for the demand that punishment should fit the crime to be interpreted with appropriate mercy. Otherwise there is room for all sorts of theories to distort justice and threaten civic peace. This will nevertheless be the case, however, when the God of justice is replaced with the god of secular humanism, as has occurred in many nations now.

To dismiss a person's account of their experience, even when it is hard to believe, even if they may be lying, is potentially dangerous, because that would encourage the temptation to make premature judgements which would seriously interfere with true justice. Of course, discernment is necessary, and people who do not have a living relationship with God will lack the benefit of his guidance.

One of the first exchanges between a newly born child and the mother is the loving acceptance, and the appropriate disposal, of the child's excreta. This provides a fundamental lesson, namely that whatever comes out of a person can be put in its rightful place in this world. The principle is worth extending to every personal relationship. Rejection, dismissal, or legalistic insistence upon correct behaviour, without the availability of compassion and room for healing may confirm a person in bitterness and recidivism. It can even make a person ill. Encouraging mutual accountability, in a kindly but truthful way, amongst credible people who can be trusted, provides opportunity for change and healing. Therefore it is best always to engage with the experiences and perceptions of others, even though they may sometimes be difficult to understand. This will naturally be associated, in both listeners and speakers, with emotions, meanings and interpersonal attachments of one sort or another. Experience and perception always involve associated emotions, and qualifications, and thoughts, and behaviours, and dependencies, all of which depend upon the person's past experience, and all of which are lived out in new circumstances in the present. If people genuinely meet in Jesus' name, and provided there be adequate truth speaking and safety, change will be allowed, prejudices dissolved and there will be hope and healing. The only safe light, however, comes from accepting what Jesus accomplished on the cross. Any other light will eventually prove to be darkness and trouble and death. If what comes to light is laid before God in Jesus' name, healing and freedom will come.

A person's experience is that person's individual experience, and no one can rightly deny it. The facts of their experience cannot rightly be rejected unless they can be shown clearly to be lying. The point is that the Spirit of truth will give discernment, which can sometimes conflict with majority opinion, and even with learned opinion. This Spirit of the living God may also change individual perception of personally experienced facts. If the facts of a person's experience are released to come to light in relationship with trusted people, whether those people are mothers, fathers, brothers, sisters, professionals, or disinterested others, and if those facts are accepted as what is so far apparent for that person, it may help the process of change and healing. In practice it often does so. Indeed, simply bringing personal experiences and perceptions to light in conversation with non-judgemental people in a secular culture often sheds new light upon them, which may be sufficient to change perception.

Assimilation of experience into character only begins to become healthily completed, however, when past and present experience is made right with God. In Psalm 85 it says that righteousness and peace kiss each other. Real Christians know this to be true from their experience. The most wholesome personal maturity comes from bringing the peace of God to our minds, souls and bodies authentically without hypocrisy through allowing every detail of thought to fall into a relationship with him in accordance with his word. This cannot be achieved by obeying rules of law, nor by simply trying to behave properly. It cannot be achieved without allowing him to heal our personal past in detail, and feeling it all in his loving presence.

Then God can heal the gaps in comprehension, and can make sense of any madness. He can renew the mind and heal overwhelming damage, He says so.[12]

Moses taught how we are made in God's image. The Spirit of Torah, the first five books of the Bible, tells how it is with God. What is called his law was given to the people of Israel in the hope that the nature and person of their God might become apparent to them so they might love him and therefore conform themselves to his likeness. The Torah of Moses was a step along the way that God was taking in order to make a people for himself, a holy nation. When the people tried to obey legalistically they were not able to do so, because mostly they did not have the Spirit to enable them to dwell in God's presence with love and understanding.

But now the Spirit comes to us after we simply accept with thankful hearts the redemption that God's only begotten son Jesus won for us when his blood was shed for us, and when he was crucified and ascended back to

---

[12] Luke 18:27; Romans 12:1-3.

his Father. Then we receive a new nature from him. And thereafter we may constantly feed on his body and his blood. So the kingdom of heaven becomes available to us. In this kingdom there is abundant everlasting life, without sickness, confusion or pain. We can tap into this abundance here in this world.

Jesus fulfilled Torah for us so that we may be changed to be like him, healed and equipped for the place he has for us. The Spirit of the Torah of Moses touches us with our maker's instructions. As we come to love him and heed him his order comes into our lives for real, with peace into our minds and souls and bodies.

This does not usually happen all at once. It is a process that takes time and may sometimes be messy. Healing may need to be radical and the changes big. We usually need other people to help us by being present for us in spirit and truth and we need the community of kingdom people.

Churches that are loaded with religious rules, trying to convey an impression of Christian perfection that any intelligent person can see to be full of hypocrisy, will never be good enough for people to be real enough to make sense of their experience, and truthfully sort out their lives with God. The necessary personal work can only be done in relationship with authentic people you can trust and believe in, who have themselves come through to new life and maturity in the kingdom of heaven and know what is involved through their own personal experience.

Healing of the facts of experience, and of the effects of living in this world, should be happening all the time in the fellowship of God's people, as happened all the time around the Lord Jesus. Healing for those who loved him resulted not only from what he said and what he did but, more than that, from knowing him and allowing him into the heart, and loving and following him.

A person who is said to be of wide experience is presumed to be someone who has seen a lot and come to terms with it all, who can handle himself or herself in many different situations, and who has learned sufficient wisdom to be trusted to do a job well. Such a person may perhaps be trusted in leadership and be worth believing in.

But people in general will be found surprisingly willing to follow anyone who offers explanations and answers. So people actually find themselves on all sorts of different paths. In effect they will be worshipping a variety of gods, and the maturity they achieve will reflect the character of the deity they effectively worship. The one who says, "I am a self-made man and I worship my creator," will certainly be full of pride. But the one who has allowed the God of Israel to heal experience, perception and memory through the cross of Jesus, applying the blood of Jesus in every detail, will be a person of genuine love, joy, peace, patience, kindness, goodness, faithfulness, gentleness and self-control, trustworthy, reflecting the presence of the Lord. That is the only one who can be sufficiently trusted.

We grow in holiness by the grace of God through experience of this world. The fellowship of other disciples of the Lord Jesus Christ needs to be good enough to assist the development of Christian maturity.

Chapter 2 – Including God

You engage with reality through your feelings, through your thoughts and through what you do. When you fully engage, in truth, and including the love of God, your feelings, thoughts and behaviour are concretely involved together, with significant relevance. Then you will be unreservedly present and peacefully aware. Meeting with others will be authentic.

But awareness can be disengaged; and it is possible to be only partially present. And the truthfulness of perception may be hindered, either for reasons you know about or for reasons you do not know about. Meeting can have reservations.

You can also escape from reality by taking an easy way out, such as by not thinking about particular aspects, cutting yourself off from particular feelings and emotions, interesting yourself with diversions, having something else on your mind, displacing your attention, or readily allowing yourself to be distracted. Music, film, sport, the computer, the latest mobile gadget, or other exciting things will always cater for your ambivalence. Social networking of one sort or another can easily keep you locked into a web of virtual reality with others who can't manage actually to come down to earth. The buzz of insouciant chatter may fascinate for ages without any need to wonder about what may be avoided. If the interest or entertainment you choose expresses something of the resistance you have to the thoughts and emotions you have denied yourself the privilege of experiencing directly, the vicarious thrills will seem all the more compelling.

Or you can concentrate on taking a disinterested and objective view of phenomena that fascinate you, study the apparent facts and research the known evidence and history, read various people's thoughts about it all, and immerse yourself in the relevant science and develop it further. This is the academic way. If you become a specialist, social esteem accrues, with financial rewards. Individual clients, firms and institutions, courts of law, and even governments, may seek your expertise and act on your evidence. You can become learned and proud. But if truth be known, your understanding will most probably be abstract and sceptical, and you may well have secret doubts and insecurities about many of your relationships, even though you may feel very certain of all your methods and facts.

After all, engaging directly with reality and relating directly with other people can be a very uncertain business, and not as simple as it seems. You need more than information: you need security in your own soul. Apparent reality can be distorted by unseen influences, by the spirit in which evidence is interpreted, and by limitations of fallen human nature.

We can make fools of ourselves rather easily. We are often disbelieved, often puzzling to others, often ridiculed behind our backs, and sometimes even bullied for who we are. If you are interested to do so, it takes time to get to know someone; but of course there may be aspects of some people you would rather not know about. And it is easy to draw wrong conclusions through pressure to conform to popular expectations.

In consequence, most people are more guarded and suspicious than they seem. They do not even need to make their upper lip especially stiff. From an early age they have learned to cope with the insecurity of uncertainty by adopting acceptably nonchalant behaviour and judging by social stereotypes according to liberal fashion, and dismissing any possibility of more accurate discernment. After all, other people may take advantage of your vulnerability if you should be at all disconcerted by feelings or embarrassing thoughts or if you stand out from the crowd because you are different. So you deny feelings of insecurity.

Sticking your head in the sand, like an ostrich, in order to dissociate yourself from certain aspects of reality is part of human nature. If you are concentrating on doing something it is always necessary to dissociate yourself from distractions. But there are many people, insecure for whatever reason, who will habitually dissociate themselves without realizing they are doing so. This uses nervous energy that is constantly defending them against full concrete engagement. And the reason is usually not obvious, although it clearly serves the purpose of protecting the person and making the person guarded and suspicious in certain respects.

This is a cause of internal stress, and can be a cause of illness. Essentially this comes from not including God, not having done the necessary business with him. Surely it is the duty of Christian churches to help people find healing, to help them bring God into the areas of their lives that are dissociated and stressed, areas of their lives they may not even know about but God knows about, in order to present the gospel in a way that is relevant to what is really going on for them, so that people may develop substantial faith for every aspect of their lives.

Such stresses come from relationships in this present world that have not properly included almighty God – not only in the present generation but also in what has been inherited from past generations. Detailed knowledge about the healing of personal relationships should be included in the equipping of Christian leaders, and should not be left to secular psychiatrists and psychologists. The phenomenology and vicissitudes of personal relationships as here described should therefore be taken seriously by Christians. Kingdom healing is available in the name of the Lord Jesus. The job of the secular medical professions is the application of cures using medical science. But there is more to healing than secular science can comprehend and kingdom healing should be used knowledgeably in a complementary way.

If your natural thoughts and feelings in response to what seems to be going on are embarrassing or troubling, or even overwhelming, who will really encourage you to discover and to face the truth? Who has the necessary breadth of understanding and generosity of spirit to gain your respect and help your healing and avoid making you feel condemned?

There are many people who may find it difficult to accept your opinions, or your criticisms, or your confusion, or your meekness, or your oddity, and who may impatiently put pressure on you to accept their conclusions, their way of seeing things, their version of reality, instead of your own, before you have actually had time to digest your experience and make sense of everything for yourself. But who will actually help you to discover your own godly truth for yourself?

And then again, if your thoughts and feelings are rather unacceptable to other people, or perhaps treated with incomprehension and blank stares, or even worse, you may quite soon learn not to admit to having them. Otherwise you could be rejected, and become rather isolated, lonely, alienated and even quite lost. In that case you could try to regain some acceptance by trying to conform to what seems to be expected by putting on a socially recognizable act of some suitable sort, and then you could try to live with your inauthenticity either until it becomes habitual or until you can no longer do it. If the acting becomes habitual you may eventually lose contact with your authentic self, or come to feel you actually have no authentic self. In this case you may as well accept privately that the culture you are living in is alien for you and has no room at all for your way of seeing things. Then you could easily become a rebel - or others may consider you to be one, whether you are one or not. And of course this begs the questions, "How should we judge authenticity?" and "What is truth?" But there may be some other people somewhere who are sympathetic towards you, or there may be some subculture somewhere that seems to understand your version of truth, and you will be able to tell whether or not they really do understand by whether or not you find some peace in your heart when you are with them.

It is a sad fact, however, that both the world and the church are full of people whose discernment and wisdom eventually prove inadequate in such circumstances, so much so that other people may eventually drive you even to doubt the veracity of your own experience - even to the extent of denying it and of not even being aware of it, and so losing touch with yourself. You could even go mad. When you really think about it in this way, it may seem surprising that most of us seem so sane.

People not only need other people but they also need God in order to find enough truth to make sound enough sense of the world and heal their madness. In a crisis our understanding may be shaken severely, and often other people can help us pull through. But sense made only with other human beings often lets us down once more, in the future, when we discover that deeper issues may not have been resolved. Those of us who have become more deeply conscious of our own human failings, and who have called upon God and become aware of his replies, discover a way of making sense of our experience that proves more substantial. Usually we have done this at a time when other people have been found wanting, and when we have been brought to our knees by conflicts or difficulties, and have been made aware of our own personal regrets and inadequacies.

God honours such repentance by healing and changing us. But friends are needed to confirm God's work.

If we live with this sort of humility before God, and trust his guidance and find godly encouragement, our vision changes so that we see in the light of his truth and see what he is doing. Then what is going on makes better sense. But our eyes also become opened to the horrifying extent to which unbelief confounds fallen human nature, and to the painful mess folk so often live in. We may then begin to see that trouble comes to so very many people from failing to include the God of truth, failing to be aware of his constant presence, failing to accept the Lord Jesus, failing to perceive in his Spirit, failing to know his words in Scripture, failing to listen to him, and failing to act on what he says.

The phenomenology of how things and events and relationships can go astray, or alternatively how they hold together from a true Christian perspective,[13] must exclude both religious tradition[14] and also secular academic systems of thinking.[15] Christian traditions are compromises either with unbelief or with other religions, often with both. Academic systems are theoretical and do not include the wisdom of spiritual experience, and are therefore abstracted and to some extent out of touch with true reality. Both tradition and academic discipline create institutions which define them in order that they may have a distinct place in political negotiations. Of course this may offer some

---

[13] Colossians 1:17.
[14] Mark 7:6-8.
[15] 1 Corinthians 1:19-21; 3:19; etc.

protection for the activity of the Holy Spirit; but in truthfully describing the vicissitudes of Holy Spirit academia and tradition are essentially irrelevant.

Jesus did not come to make institutions. He seeks personal disciples who know him and who maintain the relationship in all circumstances. Christian institutions so very often obstruct such discipleship and quench the Spirit by making rules and adapting to secular culture in the struggle to please people and survive financially. Consequently they often fail to know and reveal the mind of God sufficiently for effective healing and godly change to take place in the lives of individuals who join them. They become stuck in encouraging people to remain merely nominal Christians by adhering to church traditions, and they will often actively prevent moves of the Holy Spirit without really knowing what they are doing, and justify their actions in religious language which tempts people who really do have the Spirit of God living in them to doubt their own faith.

When reason takes the place of beginning to know the person of God through Jesus, we readily become locked into analysis of apparent facts, and into addictive attitudes toward fascinating things of this world. We may become very clever at making and doing useful things and using science and technology for our apparent benefit. And we influence institutional churches into conformity with worldly political aims and complicity with the politics of social welfare. We may have become very clever at theological debate; but this will not be sufficient for us to have authority over the powers of this world and of the flesh and of the devil. Spiritual maturity cannot be achieved through study and reason alone. Revelation comes from the god we affectively worship; and it is an essential component for creativity, healing and personal growth. Revelation is to be tested not by reason but by prophets who have a constant living relationship with God through the Spirit of God living in them. The Bible says, "...where the Spirit of the Lord is there is freedom."[16] And Jesus says, "The Spirit gives life; the flesh counts for nothing."[17]

Therefore it behoves the Christian to be sceptical about the ultimate value of the progress of academic reasoning, but not to be sceptical about salvation through accepting the Lord Jesus Christ. And no apology need be made for preaching.

Kurt Gödel was a respected academic mathematician, and an influential friend of Einstein's and (although he was not a practising Christian) Gödel's theories seem to indicate that we should look beyond the horizon of the material world for sufficient understanding. The best layman's interpretation of Gödel's mathematical 'incompleteness theorems'[18] seems to be that all formal systems of logical thought, including mathematics, are incomplete. But Scripture of the Christian tradition says of God and his only begotten Son Jesus, "He is before all things and in him all things hold together."[19] And Scripture also says, "...when he, the Spirit of truth,

---

[16] 2 Corinthians 3:17.

[17] John 6:63.

[18] Douglas Hofstadter (1979) *"Gödel, Escher, Bach: An Eternal Golden Braid."*

[19] Colossians 1:17.

comes, he will guide you into all truth."[20] Note that the word of God does not say that we shall know all the facts we need to fix things without him, but that it implies, rather, that Holy Spirit will guide us into the person of God, who knows all things[21] and in whom all things hold together. Jesus told us Holy Spirit is imparted by drinking from Jesus when you are thirsty, like a baby at your mother's breast.[22]

This book is written by a fallible human being who follows Jesus. Although there is no claim to be totally right with God, some disciplined perseverance has indeed been involved in the hope of making it so. And the book makes no pretence at being complete. It only offers godly ways of thinking about certain personal issues. Perhaps it may save some people from being deluded by wisdom of this world, however, and lead them closer to the creator of the universe, who is the God of truth who heals.

Our understanding of the word of God and the teaching of the Lord Jesus Christ has been contaminated through the centuries by pathways of reasoning and thinking that interfere with true healing. The world, the flesh and the devil have been allowed to confound godly truth. Therefore the intention of the author is to open up to the gospel of the Lord Jesus Christ areas of personal life that are in fact covered in Scripture but which have been skewed and confused by other commonly accepted

---

[20] John 16:13.
[21] 1 John 3:20; John 14:6.
[22] John 7:37-39.

ways of thinking, particularly classical Greek thinking and Enlightenment thinking.

The author has spent quite a large part of his life attending to sick people as a Christian medical doctor. He was always trying to understand the nature of personal troubles and diseases from a spiritual as well as from a scientific perspective. Doctors learn the basic science and technology at medical school, and then they begin to apply it as they attend personally to suffering people. Then the more sensitive doctors soon learn that there seems to be more to it all than science. Thereafter young doctors often find themselves moved in the direction of some specialization or other, according to natural inclination. Some become scientists. Others develop the arts of professional and personal attendance upon the sick as best they can, which commonly involves compromises with the demands of state controlled health care. A surprising number leave the profession altogether because they have not found an acceptable way to effect the necessary compromise.

I chose psychiatry, rather naively, because I enjoyed productive conversations with people stuck in various sorts of psychological torment. I enjoyed reaching better understanding with them and people responded well. But I discovered quite soon that the accepted theories and techniques of orthodox psychiatric and psychological management were not necessarily conducive to actual healing. So I went back to earning my living in general medical practice again, but at the same time I embarked on a long and arduous training in psychoanalytic psychotherapy. At the end of that time I was accredited as safe to practise; but I was frustrated.

Neither my theoretical studies nor my personal training analysis had given me sufficient understanding for peace with God. One day I got down on my knees and cried out to him for help in the name of the Lord Jesus Christ, to whom I had committed my life when I was much younger. A process of serious change and healing began from then on. Details of my own personal life, including many aspects that had been revealed through my own analysis, were put right with God. And at the same time the Holy Spirit taught me a great deal about human nature that had not been included in all the academic theory.

By the grace of God all sorts of people have chosen to open their hearts and minds with me as a medical psychotherapist. They have usually come to me because they have wanted someone to speak with in order to discover greater clarity of mind and make better sense of events and of their responses to events, and people have found healing for mental illnesses. Sooner or later, however, who I actually am inevitably became something of an influence in their lives. And my attitudes became apparent no matter how much I may have sought to hide them.

Psychotherapy, as practised by me before the days of political correctness, was not a technique applied impersonally. It was a personal relationship in which the therapist attended carefully with professional reserve, and was paid for his time rather than for his science. Although I was generally polite and tolerant, and not didactic (because I was not in the business of trying to make people better through giving instructions or prescribing rules), and although I paid attention to distortions in how I was perceived without saying very much about myself, it was impossible to be totally anonymous. And I discovered that the closer I drew in my own private life to the God of Abraham, Isaac and Israel the more some people were repelled, and some even became offensive, whilst others drew closer in understanding.[23]

Therefore I decided to declare myself to be a Christian psychotherapist, so that people would know where I stood and could avoid being offended. But then I became aware that secularists, who are the majority, do not believe that spiritual influences should play any part whatever in psychotherapy. They imagine such a relationship can be bland. So under political influence the profession has now largely become involved with opening issues out intellectually so that reasonable adjustments to attitudes and manner of living may be made without confusion or excess emotion. The process is undertaken as a calculated technique, rather than in a personal relationship in which the therapist's responses come from the disinterested compassion (or empathy) of someone who has learned relevant wisdom through finding their own healing. One consequence of this has been that the rather more disturbed and disturbing cases can no longer be held so well in the professional relationship. Consequently they go elsewhere, commonly accepting treatment with drugs. By insisting that the heart of the therapist must not so obviously be in it, professional institutions under government influence have manipulated the profession so that the

---

[23] 2 Corinthians 2:14-16.

psychotherapy undertaken these days is now done in an abstract mechanistic way rather than a personal spiritual way. Because of the lack of authenticity demanded by political correctness the profession has been dumbed down so that healing is not even an issue.

It became impossible for me to keep my integrity as a Christian whilst in secular professional employment. It was incorrect to quote the Bible or to involve God openly. Criticism was punitive. Now, therefore, I have no worldly position.

At the same time I have become aware of the extent to which secular health and welfare services are increasingly failing to bring real healing to people who suffer, despite alarming increases of financial expenditure.[24] Consequently I have come to the conclusion that it is artificial to assume that attending to people's troubles should be left solely to scientifically trained professionals, and that it is time for many more Christians to absorb the psychodynamic and spiritual insights that are relevant to the kingdom of God. Many such insights will actually be found to bring Scripture to life and reveal pertinent meaning, although they may challenge tradition and academic thinking. The practical relevance of healing and deliverance in the name of the Lord Jesus will nevertheless be more obvious, and therefore more readily accepted - not, perhaps, by

---

[24] Psychiatric services take 12% of the British National Health Service budget, more than any other speciality. And this National Health Service budget is always increasing as a percentage of total Government spending, and its growth far outpaces rises in Gross Domestic Product.

religious people, nor by academics, but rather by desperate people who do not know where to turn.

Other Christian professionals involved with intimate details of others' personal lives would no doubt be able to offer a similar personal history. So rather than calling for the welfare state to be changed, or perhaps endeavouring to change it from within, it now seems to be time to call upon Christians to open their eyes to the extent to which they are rendered insensitive to the issues, and insensible, by the hypnotic effect of the comforts offered by secular humanist application of medical and social welfare, and to the relevance of the words of God for the solution.

Chapter 3 - Fallibility

So why are so many smart people so dim? It is a common complaint! Politicians make some bad laws. Leaders dishonestly manipulate their people. Businesses go bust. Promises are not kept. Investments become worthless. Intelligent people borrow too much and determine value only by how much they can get for their money. Clever folk allow their lives to be controlled by addictions. Educated, sophisticated parents mess up their children's lives. Media mislead us. Bias is everywhere. Respectable academic studies distort the relevance of facts. People who claim to be Christian may not be followers of the real Lord Jesus Christ at all. Churches fail to preach the gospel. And that is the face of common iniquity that is actually presentable.

If you are not very careful, people can really screw you up. Too many screwed up people can cause trouble. There can be a big price to pay for being dim. Many people think we are heading for disaster.

Good things happen as well, of course, but it is undeniable that none of us gets it right all the time. We are more biddable than we like to believe, and more stubborn in justifying our failings. We are easily led into making bad decisions and failing to perceive mistakes. Trusting what ultimately proves worthless is like investing in the South Sea Bubble.

To be deceived proves surprisingly easy. Some of our mistakes are simple, like missing the nail and hitting your thumb with the hammer. But other mistakes become apparent only after many other events have become associated with them, causing complex distortions of truth. Like Pilate, many people ask, "What is truth?" All that is commonly obvious is that lack of truth makes life a misery.

Very frequently, nevertheless, we have to take the risk of trusting those in charge. If you climb aboard a bus you must trust the driver. We trust the dentist to drill our teeth. We trust the lawyer to defend us in court. We trust the doctor to treat us properly, and the midwife to deliver the baby. We trust the electrician with the wiring and the builder with the building. We trust politicians to manage national and regional affairs. You cannot do everything yourself. Inevitably we rely on others for all sorts of things. And we hope those who profess authority in their particular areas will have sufficient integrity, skill and wisdom for our trust in them to be justified.

It can be especially hard to accept that those we trust with particularly vital matters may also sometimes make mistakes. Constant practice, updating skills, and fear of litigation, may help to keep professionals efficient, but still things sometimes go wrong. Let us be honest and face the fact that we human beings are all fallible, even the experts. And human failings may cost lives. And the bitterness and retaliation of victims may also cost lives.

"No man can redeem the life of another or give God a ransom for him – the ransom for a life is costly, no payment is ever enough...," says the psalm.[25] Financial compensation is never entirely adequate for such loss; compensation only becomes truly adequate if there is forgiveness. And sometimes a person may say they forgive when true forgiveness is not in their heart.

The wisdom of the wise says forgiveness is divine, and the ability to forgive comes by the grace of God. But it is also a personal matter of willingness. Being willing to forgive involves yielding to a recognition that we are all fallible, all of the same imperfect kind. Therefore it involves an element of kindness. Without it, unhealed emotions eat away at our peace of mind. Bitterness and fear easily take hold. They trap us and can make us ill. Such is human nature! We are all sinful. There is iniquity in every one of us.

This can become a desperate business. But the Bible is very practical. It says there is no forgiveness without the shedding of blood. "The life... is in the blood...it is the blood that makes atonement for one's life."[26] And Jesus' blood was shed at his crucifixion to make atonement for us and redeem us.[27] He overcame the powers of death and of this world and of fallen human nature and of Satan and rose from the dead. He won the very greatest spiritual victory for us. Those who confess their sin and personally accept Jesus' redemption and say, "Thank you!" knowing they never deserved such mercy, become

---

[25] Psalm 49:7-9.
[26] Leviticus 17:11.
[27] Hebrews 9:22 & 9:26-28.

released from the trap of sin. They are saved out of it and have the ability, if they will use it, to continue to be saved like that. Knowing themselves forgiven, they receive the ability to forgive without incurring shame.[28] Releasing their feelings to God and asking him to heal them, they come eventually into peace of mind. The perfect Spirit of God comes into them and begins a process, if they prove willing, of perfecting and equipping them for their place in his kingdom, by teaching them to overcome as Jesus did. And most of us are such a mess that this process may take quite a while, usually a lifetime.

People who live saved and who keep on being saved, who keep on forgiving and being forgiven and putting their lives right with God, people who live in Jesus and who are devoted to him, and trust that all that happens to them is in God's hands, may not make as many mistakes as some other people; but they may still trip on the pavement, or worse.

These days, moreover, whether we like it or not, we are caught in a web of complex operations managed by science and technology and manipulated by academic thinking. We do not manage the normal course of our lives from day to day without computers and machines, technical support services, and systematic persuasion relayed by the media, which we are invited to trust on pain of social exclusion. Indeed, most people seem actually to prefer to trust machines rather than other people, although they may not always like to admit it.

---

[28] *"The vilest offender who truly believes That moment from Jesus a pardon receives"* – words in a hymn by Frances van Alstyne.

Most people seem privately to believe they would be safer if workers were replaced by robots, and the majority seem to accept that all the world's problems are best managed through scientific technology. In practice we even concur with the belief that if only we could discover all the right formulae there would be endless prosperity. Enormous grants of money go to universities in the hope of finding the means for that end.

Although unforeseen circumstances, storms, droughts, earthquakes, famines, epidemics, wars, may upset our plans, we keep on trying to be in control.

Money can be borrowed not only to provide for the necessities of life but also for schemes to try to make the world a better place and for meeting demand for the technology to make life more convenient and pleasurable. People who have capital want to benefit from it and want an income from it, and many, but by no means all, are greedy. Some want power or prestige and what people want can be manipulated. There are many unscrupulous people. Individuals and groups who do not think very deeply can easily be persuaded to accept what feels, or what superficially seems, to be good. Meeting the demands made by people for goods and public services involves borrowing and consequent indebtedness; otherwise there could be civil unrest. When debt becomes so enormous that it cannot be repaid, and when trust in other people, institutions and governments declines to a low level, however, the conclusion must be drawn that most folk do not really know what or whom to believe, despite the massive investment in scientific endeavour. So trouble can be expected.

The world is full of most dreadful problems. We know from the news that poverty, ignorance, robbery, suffering, violence, terror and disease, afflict hundreds of thousands of people. We like to be made aware of such things, but hate to be involved in them. We are glad to be able to watch them on television. To be honest, we can even sometimes find it entertaining.

But to dwell with real compassion, real fellow feeling, on the experiences of those who have been unable to escape such calamities - personally to feel what they feel rather than perceive them vicariously - seems to be far too much to contemplate, and potentially overwhelming. We fear we would never know how to handle our feelings. Passively to observe, and truly to feel but not to be able to do anything, can be too much, too. Most people simply do not believe they could ever find any true meaning for such dreadful events. They ask, "Why does God allow it? How can such suffering ever have any value?" For those unable to answer such questions there is only cynical horror.

Experience feels best if it can be entertaining; but enquiry into meaning can be too distressing. So very many people think there is little or no hope of ever gaining wisdom through seeking the face of God and asking him what it all means. Most people prefer to leave meaning to be considered in the abstract by academic specialists, and most Christians accept sceptically systematic, academic language uncritically. And understanding provided by the pictorial, narrative, spiritual and prophetic language of the Bible is dismissed too readily.

We prefer never to think too deeply about unpleasant eventualities. There can seem to be too many of them. They can be frightening. They can make us feel very insecure when we cannot figure out how to understand them. Quite naturally we do all we can to control the situations we find ourselves in so as to avoid becoming victims ourselves. All we can do is give whatever practical help we can afford for those worse off than us. Money might help. We give to charities and hope it will not be misused.

But deep down we know we cannot trust people. We cannot even totally trust ourselves. And we cannot absolutely trust the world we live in. There are many unknowns. We can only persevere in our attempts to achieve sound scientific understanding and control everything. Meanwhile we shall deal with whatever distress and mess may occur as practically as we feel we should.

But it is foolish just to throw money for repairs at those eventualities that have occurred beyond our control without godly understanding of the basic faults. How mistaken it is to believe the evidence of academic and political specialists is all we need! What hubris to look no further than the horizon of experience afforded by this fallen world and fail to call on the living God and seek his face!

It is not as though God were completely unknown to folk. People in power may ignore him; academics may make a mockery of the whole idea of him; but quite a few others call on him. Many very ordinary humble people have done so for centuries, and through getting to know him they have entered into a whole new world of experience. Those with financial and political power may be too thoroughly ensnared by the dynamics of this world to behave in a godly way, but God does hear the cries and prayers of contrite hearts.[29]

Many people say they cannot believe in a god who would allow such terrible things to occur, so much pain and suffering, so much insecurity, so much deception. But such people have never made the leap of faith necessary to give their pain, their insecurity and the strongholds of their own minds to God, to put their cares on the cross. Perhaps it is not so much a leap of faith as a willingness to accept his living presence and the gift of God's son to save us. They prefer their own reckoning, and they reckon their own minds are good enough, not recognizing that their minds are simply closed. They may believe themselves enlightened, but their light is dark.[30] Their reasoning is driven by their secular experience without the Spirit of Almighty God.

Such people have little or no understanding of their own deeper emotions, and little capacity for suffering. They may be able to endure quite well in their own strength, but their hearts are closed to God. They claim to see but are blind. The control they exert both on their world and on themselves is self-imposed. They have never confessed and yielded their emotions and reactions to God and allowed God to heal them through accepting Jesus who was crucified to save them. If they were ever to do so their hearts would then be open to God, who would always be present for them. Their ears

---

[29] Psalm 51:17.
[30] Matthew 6:23.

and eyes and hearts would be opened. Their bodies would be presented to God as their living sacrifice.[31] God would send his Spirit who would give them supernatural wisdom and minister his peace and self-control.[32] Because they have not done this, their passions are relatively brittle and shallow, and controlled by unknown influences. In extreme circumstances they may lose control.

The Bible says God made us in his own image;[33] and God is love. He knew us in our mother's womb (see Psalm 139). And, if we will acknowledge the fact, it is with our mothers that love first opens the heart.[34] Our mothers prepare the way for the love of God to open our hearts fully, only of course we do not see God in bodily form as we do our mothers. And between coming alive in our mother's love and rebirth in God's love our hearts naturally grow hardened by the frustrations and wounds and disappointments of this world. This is not to assert, as Rousseau did,[35] that the natural person untainted by society is without sin. Our sinful heredity goes back to the very first people who disobeyed God. It is just that our hearts become wounded and scarred by assaults and disappointments as we grow up so that we naturally defend ourselves with fear or bitterness. The love of God was such, however, that he sent his only begotten son to save us from this natural fallen state.

---

[31] Romans 12:1.
[32] Galatians 5:23.
[33] Genesis 1:27.
[34] 1 John 4:8 and 19.
[35] Jean-Jacques Rousseau (1762) *"The Social Contract."*

As we mature, the presence of another person may or may not be allowed to affect the heart. If there is no heart feeling, any exchange that occurs is cold because hearts are closed. In that case people are treated rather as objects; and often they can be offended in consequence. Offence inevitably wounds the heart unless there is healing. The more it is wounded by offence or disappointment the harder the heart becomes. A person may not even be aware of how cold they are, how heartless and unfeeling, how impersonal, because the heart only begins to feel, and to communicate those feelings to the mind, when it is safe to do so. And it is only safe when it is not going to break irretrievably or overwhelm the mind. For that to be the case it must be held well enough in love, and ultimately that love comes from God.[36] It was manifested most potently at the cross.

The fact is that it is a person - some*one* rather than some*thing* - that opens the heart. Then, however, other sentient beings really affect you. With other people it becomes possible to recognize that you are of the same kind because love has come into your heart from beyond the horizon of worldly responses. So you can be kind. The generosity of kindness is the beginning of love. Love is spiritual and is of God. Love grows both more divine and more real as each individual becomes more mature, more separate, more able and willing to carry his own load and more closely related to the God of Abraham, Isaac and Israel through the Lord Jesus.

Mere things, mere objects, moreover, are inert until given meaning by people through their use. Their

---

[36] 1 John 4:7-21.

significance is remembered, associated with various events. If objects affect you, it is because of their personal associations. Meaning is interpreted through personal relationship, which is spiritual. Meaning begins to be given to the world through the mother, even when the child is in the womb. Noetic transfer of meaning begins at conception. Even before the first recognition of pregnancy the mother has care for her child, and that care is both physical and spiritual.

Meaning is given spiritually. The spiritual dimension of knowing a person is not accessible to scientific investigation, although it may be truthfully known through language interpreted in the Spirit of truth, who is the Holy Spirit. Ordinary non-scientific language that comes from the heart is best for describing it. The best communication is not necessarily through clever words. People naturally read between the words, and the sense they make depends on their spirit.[37] In fact it is spirit that begets words, and spirit that interprets them. Gifting and abilities are embodied spiritually through living relationships.

Would we know language without love? When there is love the heart is encouraged in surprising and creative ways. And certainly it is much easier to learn to speak a foreign language if it be assimilated from others whom we hold in kind regard.

The favour and tender neighbourly love of other people who have sufficient understanding can make it safe to relate with genuine feeling. It is in this sort of atmosphere that there is the freedom for substantial

---

[37] 2 Corinthians 3:6.

healing to take place, and ideally the people need to have the self-control to contain any pain, fear or confusion that may quite naturally become apparent as hardness of heart changes into softness of heart, and opens to feeling and living relationship. Sometimes it can be painful when this happens, like cold dead fingers thawing in warmth.

Sometimes people behave strangely when they begin to come alive. They may shake, they may fall down, and sometimes they may get hold of strange ideas that are not from God. So good neighbours need to be under the influence of a divine authority strong enough to enable a person to forgive and turn the other cheek and continue to be generous to those who may seem objectionable or abusive.[38]

Sufficient empathy, love and understanding cannot be found through human nature alone. People may put on a kindly face if it seems to be in their interest, but they will not be able to go the extra mile without God's help. Human beings without divine beneficence in their hearts ultimately fail to bring sufficient neighbourly love to transcend human nature. The necessary understanding, compassion and resilience for maintaining openness and warmth of heart without complaint or gossip or further trouble must come from spiritual power beyond the human. Precisely where it comes from depends upon the spiritual power who is effectively invoked, that is upon the god that is effectively worshipped. Even Satan can appear kind if it suits him. But in the long run, to bring healing that will last, we need the personal presence of

---

[38] Luke 10:25-37.

the God of Abraham, Isaac, Jacob and Jesus to melt our hearts and give us new life by putting his Spirit in us.

Truly knowing another individual involves opening the heart so that the inner dimensions of feeling, and thought, and awareness of one's own personal behaviour, become available to experience. And although a person may become aware of another person with whom it may be good to communicate about one's inner experience with openness of heart, communication is not always easy. Understanding is not always easily shared. Quite naturally, one proceeds tentatively because difficulties concerning such sensitive matters may cause insecurity and frustration. Kindly perseverance may nevertheless give cause for conscious reflection, and gradually give rise to the development of better mutual understanding.[39]

Each individual has a spiritual presence that becomes known to a greater or lesser extent by others, and is defined as personality. Personal knowledge of another comes from the response of the heart to the presence of the other. The inner experience, thought, feeling, and awareness of one's own behavioural response, gives a measure of the other person, only some of which may be conscious. This is not a measure that can ever be truly ascertained by any mathematical or psychological measurement, or fully defined in language, although it may be known in the heart. However, it is a quality that bears some relation to truth. It is only God who knows the whole truth of a person.[40] The closer to the truth, the

---

[39] Romans 8:20-21.
[40] 1 John 3:20; Psalm 147:5.

greater the peace it brings. The heart opens to a person; but it is only when the real true Jesus has been accepted that the Spirit of truth comes to dwell in the soul and understanding becomes more mature. There is peace in that.

The God of Abraham, Isaac, Israel and Jesus knows all things, and his understanding is infinite. We have access to his mind when we accept the Lord Jesus, his only begotten son.[41] If we have his Holy Spirit and righteously seek his guidance, we are able to bring his godly understanding into issues and personal relationships that the secular world perceives with incomprehension or horror. We are able to think about facts and issues that people who do not really know the Lord deny or are unable to bear, and often we are able to interpret what is going on with a greater degree of truth than secular writers, academics and politicians.[42] We develop the empathy, compassion, and self-control, which come from having allowed the living God truly to heal our own hearts and minds.

When we personally accept that Jesus has redeemed us from our sin, our hearts are opened with gratitude. We find ourselves truly thankful from the bottom of our hearts. The Bible says our hearts are circumcised and we no longer have hearts of stone but hearts of flesh.[43] Our hearts are softened. We put pity behind us and develop

---

[41] 1 Corinthians 2:6-16, Colossians 2:2-4.

[42] 1 Chronicles 12:32; Psalm 119:99-100; Genesis 41:16; Daniel 2; Acts 8:9-23; 1 Corinthians 2:16, etc.

[43] Deuteronomy 30:6, Ezekiel 36:26, Romans 2:29, Colossians 2:9-12.

disinterested compassion with understanding. Our souls receive new life, and God, by his grace, ministers some of his understanding to us. So if we will, we may interpret our experience his way.

This does not exclude mathematical measurement or scientific facts. Rather it adds his essential spiritual dimension. The fact is that facts are always interpreted spiritually. Surely it is best to have the bearing of godly truth upon them, rather than some other spiritual influence.

There are many spiritual influences, many spiritual beings and many gods, as the ancient Greeks knew, and as many other people know too. They each have their different personalities, and have the power to influence human beings to become like them and develop their reasoning in accordance with them. Spiritual influences affect people's perception, thinking and behaviour, which in turn affect their physical health. And human behaviour has a spiritual component that influences other people subliminally. Personalities and emotions are spiritual, and there are spiritual beings that extend powerful influence over groups and whole societies. So cultures are spiritual influences. People who do not conform to a culture are not so readily understood in that society and are therefore liable to be treated with suspicion, which is uncomfortable. And they may often be rejected, even persecuted and actively cursed, and this can be felt as oppression, and can be a cause of confusion and clumsiness that may result in mistakes, addictions, abuse and torments of various kinds. Jesus became a curse for us, however, and those who call on him and accept what he has done for them have access to his healing, which is more powerful than any curses.[44]

So what we deem 'experience' includes not only sensation produced by the environment we live in but also our inner personal reactions.[45] And within the realm of 'experience' are to be included not only sensation but also thoughts, and feelings, and awareness of one's behavioural responses, and their meaning. Consequently the word 'perception' may often be more appropriate than 'experience' because it is more inclusive. Or perhaps the word 'experience' should rather be used to define perception vivid enough to be laid down in memory; for it can be argued that it is not everything actually perceived that is available for recall, and that can therefore actually be counted and laid down as 'experience'.[46]

Attempts to exclude personal reaction and inner experience from our deliberations, for example by using mathematical abstractions, systematic scientific enquiries or theoretical disquisitions, are useful for calculation. But a world that excludes personal reactions within one's own body and one's own person, is essentially unreal and out of touch, and if personal reactions are ignored too long it is possible that they may erupt in chaos or sickness, because they naturally demand to be heard and a vital element of essential sense will have

---

[44] Galatians 3:13; Luke 6:27-31.

[45] 1 John 3:11 – 4:6.

[46] This is a gloss on Maurice Merleau-Ponty's suggestion that there may be no difference between experience and perception ("*The Primacy of Perception,*" 1947).

been excluded from personal consideration. This will permit too great a degree of confusing dysfunction and overwhelming frustration into society, which can be dangerous.

When Jesus called his disciples the salt of the earth and light of the world[47] he was implying that they would bring godly influence and healing into this physical world. Their hearts would be opened with understanding, and they would spread it about.[48] This foretaste of his kingdom rule would attract other followers. But we were warned to test the spirits,[49] and we were also warned of dreadful times in the last days before his return.[50]

It follows that Christians, particularly those of Calvinist, Puritan and Reformed traditions, who have reasoned dogmatically that all sensations and emotional elements are of no use to salvation, for fear that they will promote sentimental illusions and idolatrous superstitions, have often prevented individual thoughts and emotions from being brought before the Lord day by day so that people may be healed by him and change to be more like him in their hearts. How could they understand how mad people could be reckoned amongst those predestined to be saved? Those people who have believed that any interpersonal emotional dependence represents idolatry of the flesh have quenched the working of the Holy Spirit in many

---

[47] Matthew 5:13-16.
[48] Mark 4:1-25 and 12:28-34.
[49] 1 John 4:1.
[50] 2 Thessalonians 2 and 2 Timothy 3:1-9.

people's lives because they themselves have failed to allow the Holy Spirit to have access to their own hearts and souls in order to soften and heal and change them. Minds are changed through open relationship (1 John 1:7). They have not understood that just as young children need mothers and fathers, so also grown up children need mothers and fathers too, and the most appropriate mothers and fathers, as time goes on, are not always blood relations. They have wrongly refused to present their own bodies as living sacrifices,[51] believing the flesh to be untouchable because of its fallen nature. They have not had the faith to believe human fallibility can be overcome and healed in the power of the Holy Spirit. Their religion is consequently all in their minds, and therefore inauthentic.

Undoubtedly Calvinist tradition developed from spiritually inspired new understanding the word of God. But fears of being wrong with God, in the face of oppressive opposition from other wrong teaching, seems to have made them legalistic. It seems that they were never able to give time and space to opening their own fallible hearts to the Lord and giving him their thoughts and feelings and personally waiting for his healing and instruction and direction. Instead they imposed their faulty rules, using Scripture as a rule book.

Those who believe that the glory of God and one's own salvation must always remain above the threshold of consciousness, and be subject to dogmatic reason, have failed to allow God to work in mysterious ways in

---

[51] Romans 12:1.

the human body.[52] Christians who have considered the living, physical body to be a machine separate from the soul have prevented physiology and emotion and behaviour from undergoing the processes of change necessary for substantial healing to occur. Instead they have presumed to control everything by rules. Legalistic people have prevented the healing of many illnesses through substituting didacticism, good works, and a Protestant work ethic[53] that can lead to material prosperity, for the inner working of the Holy Spirit. They have prevented many people from becoming the salt and light that changes the world because they have prevented the Spirit from instilling genuine love and truth and patience and compassion in the hearts of ordinary folk who, in their weakness, have sought the Lord for healing and for salvation in this world. They have encouraged instead a disconnection between spirit and living body, the substitution of religion for real personal knowledge of the Spirit of God, and the rise of objective scientific procedures through which people

---

[52] Richard Baxter (1615-1691) wrote, *"It is an irrational act and not fit for a rational creature to love any one further than reason will allow us… . It very often taketh up men's minds so as to hinder their love of God."* (Christian Directory, IV p.253.) It is not reason that should check us but rather the indwelling Spirit of God with whom we should be in constant communication – which is not always conscious.

[53] Protestant prosperity was significantly analysed by Max Weber in *"The Protestant Ethic and the Spirit of Capitalism"* (1904-5). It should be noted that he was referring to the Calvinist distortion of Protestantism, which was strong on didacticism but short on love of one's neighbour.

may be effectively objectified, oppressively managed and abused if they are not very careful.

The rise in the incidence of mental illness after the crusades and plagues of the later Middle Ages – a rise which continues to this day – can be seen as a consequence of the substitution of legalism for genuine spirituality. Both the Venetian physician Alvise Luisini in the sixteenth century, and Richard Baxter in England in the seventeenth, may be considered representative of many Christians throughout the centuries who have known some success in Christian spiritual healing for both psychological and physical conditions, but the connection between spirit and mind and body was poorly understood by them, and the religious practices recommended were almost always dogmatic and legalistic.[54] Sometimes physical treatment was even withheld unless confession and penance had been undertaken. Nevertheless God always keeps his promise not to snuff out a smouldering wick.[55]

From the earliest days after Jesus, many churches became preoccupied with defending themselves against the accusations and deceptions of academic and political arguments, and they consequently became institutionalized and inflexible, and developed dogmatic teaching, and failed to perceive what the Holy Spirit was

---

[54]Richard Palmer, *"The Church, Leprosy and Plague in Medieval and Early Modern Europe,"* and Michael MacDonald, *"Psychological Healing in England 1600-1800,"* in *"The Church and Healing, Studies in Church History"* Volume 19, Oxford, Blackwell, 1982.

[55] Isaiah 42:3.

saying to individuals. The work of the Holy Spirit in healing was extensively lost, and saints were not properly equipped. The authority and power of the Holy Spirit was submerged, and fear of witchcraft and magic caused any true spiritual awareness to be mocked as superstition.

Only recently has the Holy Spirit been less quenched, so as to be given more access to intimate details of individual lives again, as people have become more aware and more concerned about the inner experiences of their own souls, and their feelings and thoughts and motivation for behaviour, particularly through the work of certain philosophers and psychotherapists in the nineteenth and twentieth centuries, mentioned later in Chapter 7, working within the Judeo-Christian culture. Clergy by and large were no longer involved with the practicalities of individual souls and bodies. Scripture was applied to social theory but the personal application of scriptural understanding of mankind was neglected.[56]

Enemy spirits have risen up in competition, with the power to rearrange the spiritual influences in a person's life so as to give deceptive impressions of complete healing. Paganism, white witchcraft, and an enormous diversity of spiritual healing methods have become openly commonplace.

---

[56] H. Wheeler Robinson (1911) *"The Christian Doctrine of Man,"* Edinburgh, T. & T. Clark. Aubrey Wheeler (1949) *"The Vitality of the Individual in the Thought of Ancient Israel,"* Cardiff, University of Wales Press. C. Ryder Smith (1951) *"The Bible Doctrine of Man,"* London, Epworth Press.

Therefore people who turn to the Lord Jesus Christ need to be discerning, to resist the devil, and to accept unconditionally that Jesus took their personal sicknesses and pains and confusions and feelings and thoughts and transgressions and iniquities and punishment on the cross. And they should be simply thankful and patient, allowing themselves space and time for the Holy Spirit to work in their bodies, hearts and minds. They should attend to him carefully and allow him to give them the courage to think differently from the way the world thinks.

When our fallibility is exposed it is the opening not for legalism, nor for any method, or for any other spirit, but for the person of the Lord Jesus Christ to come in. When we are weak, then we may be strong in the power of the Lord (Luke 9:46-48, 2 Corinthians 12:10).

Chapter 4 – Perceptual Distortion

Christians who live by religious rules commonly ignore their desires and feelings. And so they also ignore all the disturbing thoughts that may accompany them, because inculcated legalism will dictate that they must always be good. They cannot believe they could ever be good with thoughts that seem bad or negative.

But the Bible says we should take captive every thought to make it obedient to Christ.[57] And we cannot take a thought captive if we deny that it is there. If we deny responsibility for it we'll refuse to be accountable for it. Instead of taking the thought captive we shall in fact have released a foe to work in the dark that should have been taken prisoner. Because we cannot bear our shame and guilt, and all our other disturbing thoughts and feelings and emotions and desires, and because we cannot bear to appear not to be complying with the respectable standards of behaviour that are expected of us, we shall have taken what seemed at the time to have been the easy option of dissociating our consciousness from our gut reactions. This habit can very easily

---

[57] 2 Corinthians 10:5.

become automatic.[58] The consequences, however, could cost us even our very life.

King Ahab released his enemy Ben-Hadad after he had conquered him in battle, when he should, instead, have understood nature of the man and the grave dangers of making a deal with him. He should have killed him according to the will of God. King Ahab should have been mature enough to allow uncomfortable truth into his mind. As a consequence of not doing so, Ahab himself met his death.[59]

We may handle this sort of thing these days by first simply accepting what Jesus accomplished for us at the cross, and then we can yield all our desires and thoughts and feelings to him, put them on the cross, and act with the courage that comes from Holy Spirit according to his direction. Jesus took our guilt, and became shame for us, and he took all our other natural reactions, too.[60] He knows about them. He was a person with flesh and blood like us. So we can freely confess to God all that is actually in our guts and hearts and minds, and thank him for Jesus. We take our thoughts captive by telling God all about them and accepting what Jesus has done. Then they are in God's hands and we are released from guilt and shame about them. We can come before God just as if we had never sinned because we have accepted

---

[58] The habit tenses the diaphragm muscle under the ribs so that the belly does not move so much when breathing. You can discover how tense your own diaphragm is if you just try to breathe deeply into your hips!

[59] 1 Kings 20:42.

[60] Isaiah 53:4-5, Hebrews 10:22, and 12:2.

Jesus.[61] Then we can act according to the will of God instead of obeying our social conscience and our fear of mankind. God sends his Spirit, and heals. Then he reveals further understanding to us, and so we find real hope, and continue to persevere. This process can go on for a lifetime. It continually sets us free from the world, and it is a much healthier habit than obeying rules and dissociating from unpleasant truth.

Sometimes, frankly, the process of getting free of all our habitual ways of dissociating from unpleasant truth takes a long time. And it can be made much longer than necessary by all the psychological deceptions and secular scientific explanations abounding in the world today that take no account of our need for God to heal us. Getting free can be quite a battle, even when we really do know what Jesus has done for us, and even when we have been baptized in Holy Spirit.

The process of healing can actually make a person feel tired and ill whilst it is going on, and it can lead them into a state of not always thinking very soundly as old ways of understanding are being changed and as God is renewing large parts of the mind. Healing is not always miraculously instantaneous, and frequently involves changes in perception. The process can sometimes even seem rather dangerous, and it can leave you feeling vulnerable for a while. But it can sometimes be a mistake to visit the doctor and to take the treatment offered, because most doctors simply do not understand the process of spiritual change, although of course they are very good at diagnosing serious illness that needs urgent

[61] Ephesians 1:7.

71

attention. Many people become addicted to prescription medicines that make them feel better when they could have overcome the problems in a better way, but perhaps not so readily, with Jesus.

So it is even possible that you may need to make arrangements for your protection, like staying somewhere safe, or changing your social activities, or perhaps talking intimately on a regular basis with someone you actually trust who is intelligent enough to be aware of the issues. Basically we all need to make the space and time to allow God always to be changing us.[62]

Sometimes it is best just to allow yourself to be depressed or to feel ill for a while, and get through it with God's guidance. And it is surprising how often people who are suffering one way or another find themselves thinking over past events, which is a natural process that helps put the past into better perspective. If allowed to run its proper course it saves a person from being stuck with faulty perceptions.[63] Prejudices, attitudes wrong with God, unhealthy conceptions and strongholds of the mind, may make us ill. But taking thoughts captive and making them obedient to Christ before it is too late can bring a person through to healing.

If you are always fighting by resisting and dismissing everything that seems frightening, uncomfortable, out of the ordinary, difficult or offensive, and if you are not listening to God, he will have no opportunity to change

---

[62] Psalm 18:19.

[63] An interesting example of taking stock and allowing change is W. H. Hudson (1918) *"Far Away and Long Ago."*

you, to heal you and to lead you on to greater maturity from one degree of glory to another. Jesus was speaking about this sort of thing when he says, "Everyone will be salted with fire."[64] All sorts of things may befall us, even most terrible things; but Jesus remains with us, and sees us through, if we have committed our lives to him. Proverbs 17:3 says, "The crucible for silver and the furnace for gold, but the Lord tests the heart." So it is our reactions that count. God tests us through everything that happens, including illness, in order to afford us opportunity to be changed in the ways we perceive and behave so as to reflect his glory better. He wants us to allow his fire to burn up the dross, which is sin.[65] Salts are the ash produced by fire. Salt was also a sign of covenant with the one true God,[66] a sign of having allowed the dross in your life to be burned up with God's fire, which is essential for adding godly flavour to your life. Our natural reactions may be understandable, but they are sinful. Yet they may be transformed, if we are willing, by constantly giving them totally to God in confession, by accepting his forgiveness, healing and guidance through Jesus, and by obeying Holy Spirit.

When understood like this, suffering means allowing God to do his work in us.[67] Through allowing God into our experience we begin to see in his way, and we gain something of his understanding. God's love is revealed to us when his presence makes it safe to open our hearts

---

[64] Mark 9:49.

[65] Hebrews 12:29, etc.

[66] As in 2 Chronicles 13:5, etc.

[67] Matthew 19:14, King James Version.

to him like children, when we tell him our thoughts and feelings and put them on the cross, and when we then receive his healing.

Everyone who has truly loved knows that love involves some suffering. We feel for the person we love, and are affected by everything that person does. And the person we love responds in a loving way to our empathy. Our loving relationship with God is like this. And as we recognize and respond to God's love for us we become more able to feel for other people, and to know more of what others feel, with godly discernment, wisdom and compassion. As God imparts his understanding we may suffer for all sorts of other people and situations, which will inform our intercession.[68] Furthermore, people may hate us for attitudes that prove right with God but that do not conform to the world, and they may persecute us one way or another. Essentially this comes from their envy.[69] And all this informs not only our prayers but also how we behave and all that we do. Christians suffer.[70] But they are able to endure their suffering and make sense of it. Because they give their natural reactions to God in Jesus' name, he takes them,[71] and sends his Spirit to comfort and to guide them and to bless others. Nevertheless, it is false to give the impression that this is always easy.

---

[68] 1 Corinthians 12:26; 2 Corinthians 1:3-11; Romans 12:15; Philippians 3:10; Isaiah 63:9; Hebrews 13:3.

[69] Matthew 27:18; Mark15:10.

[70] 2 Timothy 3:12.

[71] Isaiah 53:4-5.

Many Christians pray for the sick, in one way or another, with some success. The Holy Spirit is powerful. Certainly miracles of healing do happen when the kingdom of heaven is invoked and God is praised and worshipped, and when God is thanked for sending his only begotten son Jesus Christ, and when the great victory Jesus won on the cross is personally accepted with a grateful, open heart. Sometimes people baptized in Holy Spirit may speak into situations with authority that sets people free, although it is possible for people effectively to resist this if they want to. Natural human attitudes, prejudices and strongholds of the mind in all individuals can seriously get in the way of accepting that same resurrection, healing power which brought Jesus back from the dead.

Of course, if we ourselves should suddenly become ill we may be most dreadfully surprised. Although our physical or mental illness may seem to have come out of the blue, it may be worth considering that something might have been going on that we have been unaware of, and that has now resulted in our sickness. So perhaps we would find healing more easily if we were to ask God to help us discover the meaning, to give us revelation and show us how to suffer our way through whatever we have to face, and bring us out healed at the end of it.

Jesus not only did miracles of healing, he also taught. His teaching gave people understanding.[72] He used parables. He responded to questions and engaged in repartee. He was challenged by all sorts of people, and

---

[72] Matthew 13:15.

was generally addressed as 'Teacher,' or 'Rabbi.' But he did not teach rules. He did not tell people how to do things, but rather challenged them, in return, to love God and love their neighbours as God loved them. His example encouraged them to use the love in their hearts to love their neighbours, and to be personally accountable before God. He lived and spoke true to the word of God. He embodied the word of God, and he called disciples who loved him to follow him and feed from his very flesh and blood. He challenged them to develop understanding and to think for themselves in relation to himself and to his father. He was severely critical of traditions invented by people, and of false religion. He helped people to understand the implications of the kingdom of heaven. And what he said and did remains life-giving because he remains alive, to the extent of leading those who accept him into eternal life with him.

We should not forget, furthermore, that he spoke to Jews. He lived in a culture which had been prepared by God since the days of Adam. In that Hebrew culture there was the possibility of his words being heard, and his person taken to heart, fairly readily because of the work done by patriarchs, prophets and sages before him. And they had been prepared by John the Baptist. Therefore Jesus' teaching did not altogether fall on deaf ears. His way of understanding was not totally foreign. The way people's minds were made up did not altogether get in the way. The culture was fairly conducive to godly understanding and healing. The Jews of that time had not become as corrupted by classical Greek thinking as we have become today.

Although they spoke Greek, they continued to think as Hebrews.

Amongst us today, scepticism, suspension of judgement, relativism, reductionism, the assumption that man is the measure of all things, abstract systematic classification, and scientific enquiry, all ultimately derived from pagan classical Greece, pervade our culture. Spiritual awareness is dismissed as fanciful or unreal. Any direct, concrete response to experience is perceived with misgiving. Understanding rooted in Christian faith is mocked. People prefer to respond in calculated ways, to think carefully before they act, informed by all the facts. An extraordinary volume of factual knowledge is available to us, more than ever before, but we make of it all only things of convenience. Wisdom is undermined. Meanings that accord with the eternal word and purposes of God are rejected.

What is going on often seems confusing to many people. Frequently it seems too utterly appalling to think about. Truth for most folk is only facts. Meaning is too confusing. So what commonly passes for truth is the result of trying to ascertain as precisely as possible, through measurement, mathematical description and precise definition, how facts relate to each other. The notion that truth is the spirit of a person who interprets and gives meaning is foreign to most people. They look to sceptical, mechanistic, academic thinking and find answers they can use for immediate advantage. They look to science for salvation but merely discover ennui. And life becomes relatively meaningless.

Jesus said, "A wicked and adulterous generation looks for a miraculous sign, but none will be given it except the sign of Jonah,"[73] meaning that he himself is the sign, and like Jonah he was buried three days but rose again. What he preached was rich with truthful meaning and bore surprising fruit, more than Jonah's preaching had borne. Jesus also said, "Night is coming when no-one can work."[74] And sometimes night seems to have come. But perhaps there is still enough light for some to see. Perhaps it is still possible that some will open their ears and eyes and hearts and understand differently from the ways of the secular multi-faith world. A thread of Judeo-Christian culture still survives among us, although it is often drowned out by academia and media. We should not forget the promise that the spirit of Greece will be overcome.[75]

When we do not hear God clearly, nor see truly, nor understand his way, we do not live as God ideally intends, and our engagement with reality will be out of kilter. Our experience and perception, and our relationships and behaviour, will be subtly distorted. This must inevitably have a lasting effect on our minds and bodies, because each one of us is made in God's image.[76] Those who inherit our genes will also be affected. Commonly we fail to perceive the causes of our sicknesses and sorrows; but if we become ill maybe we should ask God how he would heal us. Maybe we should ask him to show us, and then listen to him.

---

[73] Matthew 16:4.
[74] John 9:4.
[75] Zechariah 9:13, Daniel 8:19-25.
[76] Genesis 1:27.

Our ears are often so dull, and our eyes so closed, and our hearts so calloused,[77] that our perception and discernment are misleading. Society is lost in a fog and fails to perceive this fact most of the time. God, and sin, and the truth of what is going on in the world, and of what the devil is up to, go unacknowledged. We become confused and deceived by subtly persuasive powers of darkness. And our spirits, souls, bodies and relationships often bear witness to the consequences, although that fact, too, mostly goes unrecognized.

Everything that is going on, that relates to us in any way, affects our souls and bodies to some extent. The world inside us connects with the world outside us and what goes on outside affects us within. And what goes on within us one way or another affects the people amongst whom we live and our environment. Why pretend otherwise? The stiff upper lip may be necessary sometimes, and it is wise to keep control of one's tongue, for there is no point in exposing ourselves to exploitation by other people for what they may interpret as weakness. But that need not imply that we should deny our thoughts and feelings or pretend to ourselves that they do not exist in response to events. When Jesus said we should deny ourselves he meant we should not satisfy our desires through lusting after the things of this world, but rather conform our wills to his. He did not mean that we should deny that we have those desires but rather that "we take captive every thought to make it obedient to Christ."[78]

---

[77] Isaiah 6:9-10, Matthew 13:11-15.
[78] 2 Corinthians 10:5

Sometimes our responses to events may eventually make us ill. How we respond depends on how we perceive, make sense of things and understand. Responses that make us ill reveal hitches and glitches and lack of freedom in our spirits and souls and living bodies. Some of these hitches and glitches become ingrained and inherent. Therefore we need to be set free in Jesus' name from such impediments. Then our physiology and our behaviour will also be freed. Sometimes our minds need to be set free first; and sometimes our minds seem to get free only after our bodies and souls. Deliverance and understanding go hand in hand. God's healing is a process that involves the whole of us, and it is artificial for us to separate spirit, soul and body. Only the Holy Spirit can do that, and he will only do it for his own purposes.[79]

When we accept the Lord Jesus Christ and receive Holy Spirit and are healed we become much more able to perceive relevant, true facts about what is, and what has been, going on, and to put them in true perspective so that we act with godly wisdom,. He is the only one with the power truly to set us free to be like this.[80] That was implied when Jesus said he is the truth.[81] However the Spirit of God can operate without our awareness, and he can be doing things within us that we are not conscious of. And quite often he uses people who are not actually wholly devoted to him. And he can override our

---

[79] Hebrews 4:12.
[80] Acts 4:12.
[81] John 8:32 & 14:16.

consciousness and lead us into his truth in spite of ourselves.

It follows that the notion of truth that a person has is a function of the god (the spiritual person) whom that person effectively worships. Truth is a spiritual power, the presence and influence of a spiritual being, influencing how an individual makes sense of experience. To some extent, therefore, different versions of truth will prevail in different religions and in their cultures and societies. Because different gods are worshipped different nuances and meanings will attach to events. The outworking of events, and all their interconnections, will produce different cultures according to the presiding deity. History, to be true, would include the story from God's perspective of all the various outcomes.

Since every human being is made in the image of the one true God of Abraham, Isaac and Israel, and since we each live in the world he created, however, we each have a common awareness of common objects. Names and details of objects can be universally recognized. A piece of cloth is a piece of cloth the world over, although variously named according to the language used. And things are in lifeless relationship with other things. For example, various pieces of cloth and buttons and cotton thread and padding are brought together in a particular form of relationship to make a coat. But the fact of such purely physical relationship is only perceived by living beings. It is the use to which objects are put, and the meanings given to what people do with them, and to events that involve them, that will differ. And they will differ in implication according to the extent that uses and meanings are influenced by the deity worshipped. So the coat may be part of a uniform or a winter warmer, an object of pride or an object of mockery. The interpretation of facts and events is influenced by the nature and qualities of the presiding deity, that is, by the personality of that spiritual being. The personal imprint of the god will affect the conduct of events in the society of people influenced (whether wittingly or unwittingly) by that god. And it will have consequences intended by that spiritual being. Deities are more powerful than human beings. And Jesus Christ is Lord of lords.[82]

Some persons are seen; some are not seen. Divinities do not have material bodies, although their presence may be perceived by inference, much as the wind is perceived by waving branches of trees. People sometimes try to make their influence more pronounced by representing the personalities of their gods artistically, and making images, idols or totems to represent them; and although the images are not in fact the spiritual beings represented they can be powerful reminders, and can have a fearful impact unless they are recognized as the illusions and deceptions they are, Spiritual influences affect every aspect of our engagement with reality. Our behaviour and expressions are affected by them. All other spiritual influences may be trampled down under one's feet in the name of the

---

[82] Jeremiah says these deities that I have called gods are not gods. I have no quibble with Jeremiah. Of course they are illusions and deceptions. But they do have spiritual power that deludes people. (See Jeremiah 10:1-16; 16:19-20).

Lord Jesus Christ of Nazareth. But to wield such authority the Lord Jesus must be truly known as Lord.

The words we have for facts, relationships and events are used differently, and have slightly different implications and meanings, under different spiritual influences. A common example is the word 'charity,' which has commonly taken on a secular meaning although it comes from a word which originally meant 'loving grace.' Another example is the word 'gay,' which has taken on a sexual meaning although it used to mean 'carefree.' Another is the element '-phobia,' which used to indicate 'fear' is now used to describe resistance to imposed dogma. So the meaning of words can even be intentionally distorted and used by political pressure groups to manipulate the way people think, and the manipulation may be reinforced by the subtle threat of sanctions.

Of course, words do change their meaning over time to some extent, according to shifts in culture,[83] but such evolution of meaning differs from the intentional imposition of meaning-change for political ends. The extent to which cultural changes, reflected in shifts in the gradual meaning of words, may be the consequence of unconscious avoidance of godly truth about disturbing facts, could be an interesting Christian philological study. Such avoidance is not usually wilful. Seeing things in the true light of Jesus and knowing the mind of God about them is not possible for those who have not received his Spirit to know him. And in this context it is

---

[83] See e.g. Daniel Heller-Roazen (2005) "*Echolalias – On the Forgetting of Language,*" New York, Zone Books.

noteworthy that the Koran inverts the meaning of many Bible passages that were written before it. It is also relevant that there are nominal Christians who read the Bible in alternative ways, including substitution of 'mother' for 'Father,' and of 'the church' for 'Israel,' and even of 'Satan' for 'God,' and who consequently fail to understand not only the relevance of the Old and New Testaments but also the continuing relevance of the Jews and the nation of Israel as God's chosen people.

Therefore it seems reasonable to assert that if ungodly inference is to be avoided, and if what is meant is to be conveyed, the language used should not only bear a truthful, godly relation to the original meaning of the combined words, but should also be sensitive to the spiritual influences in the culture of those being addressed but nevertheless uncompromising.

Just about everyone will agree that it is legitimate to study actual things, and inert facts of physical relationships of material objects, by the methods of systematic science. The results are often extremely useful. But the abstraction and objectification requisite for mathematics and scientific enquiry inevitably result in scepticism, ennui and unreality if applied to whole, living human beings. If these methods are applied to the personal dynamics of feelings, thoughts and behaviour, or to interpersonal relationships, or to spiritual worship, they inevitably fail adequately to describe the spiritual dimension of living relationship. Meaning in living relationship cannot be fully known if it is only objectified. Although it can be signified, it can never be adequately or fully described in an abstract way, and therefore it can never be adequately understood scientifically. People instinctively know this. They dislike being objectified, and rightly feel manipulated if they are treated impersonally, simply as data. Therefore there are obvious limits to the efficiency of the sciences of psychology and sociology for psychiatric management, business, politics, social administration and true justice.

The dimension of living relationships requires spiritual wisdom rather than scientific knowledge. It is necessary to have spiritual discernment to see what is going on clearly. Without sound judgement based in experience whose meaning has been integrated into the living body, soul and mind, it will not be possible for a person to know the true implications of living events. These qualities are not instilled by knowledge acquired as data, as matters purely of fact. Meaning is acquired through relationships, which are spiritual, with other people and other spiritual beings of whom the whole is greater than the perceivable parts. We make sense of what is going on because the sense others have made of relationships, guided by the influences upon them (ultimately by their god) has been revealed to us in the past, and has affected us. Revelation of meaning comes to us when there is mutual love, acceptance and recognition. And language comes from this. When we are loved and known, we ourselves become able to love and to know. Unless we respond emotionally we do not gain meaningful experience. Unless our feelings and thoughts are made right with God our understanding will not be godly and our wisdom will ultimately be inadequate.

We take in and give out not only through our orifices but also though our hearts spiritually. The effect others have on us affects our behaviour, which has spiritual influence as well as physical effect. Neither science nor mathematics nor theory can adequately comprehend this spiritual dimension.

Reality is experienced physically and made sense of spiritually. Whether they know it or not, everyone is subject to spiritual influence. Spirit brings names of things to mind and interprets relationships. Furthermore, if we will allow it to do so, spirit engages memory stored in the living physical body, and also imagination, to bring revelation and understanding.[84] This is how ideas develop and how the mind changes. The sense we make of experience determines how our minds are formed and made up, how we make our way through life, how our bodies behave, and even the illnesses to which we succumb.

Whom we worship is crucial. For protection, therefore, it behoves a person to guard against dangerous spiritual influences.[85] The only benign God is the God of Abraham, Isaac and Israel, the person whom Jesus called Father, and only with the Lord Jesus is it safe to perceive truth in his presence.

In Christian cultures in the past there were many doctors and nurses who to some extent used to assume this sort of thing without thinking much about it. But in countries where statutory health care has now become

---

[84] I have described this process more fully in my book *"Healing for the Wounded Life."*

[85] Proverbs 4:23.

secularized, such godly understanding has been banished.[86] Even the compassion of loving one's neighbour as one's self seems to be becoming rather scarce as nursing staff become technologists.

Therefore it seems to be time for spiritual aspects of healing, and spiritual aspects of the nature of mankind assumed in the Bible, now to be adopted effectively by lay people who belong to the kingdom of heaven. And it is time for Christian healing to complement technological healing for those who seek it.

Christians would be wise to make the effort carefully to discern secular perceptual distortions in areas of life hitherto considered safe and, with gentle compassion and from a scriptural perspective, to make constructive criticism of attitudes and language. The protection and healing of those God brings to his kingdom depend upon the watchfulness of the shepherds.

---

[86] The American Medical Association insists doctors must practise only scientifically.

Chapter 5 - Abstraction

Surely the salvation offered by the Lord Jesus Christ applies to the whole person, spirit, soul and body.[87] In this respect it seems totally unreasonable for spirit and soul to be held to be separate from a person's living body. Really it behoves everyone, and most especially those who attend the sick, to consider the whole person, and not to try to address the soul or the body or the mind or the spirit alone, as abstractions.

Scientific medicine addresses only the sickness. It searches for physical causes and disregards spiritual affairs, as indeed it must if it is to compromise with a diversity of different faiths and treat them all as having equal power and authority. But if as Christians with Holy Spirit living in us we search for godly understanding we shall discover that there are spiritual issues relating to what we conceive to be physical sicknesses, and there are physical issues relating to spiritual and mental sicknesses, and the soul is always involved.

Understanding about experiences of sickness and suffering, therefore, should not be the preserve solely of

---

[87] 1 Thessalonians 5:23.

medical science. Spiritually aware people should also be involved. Please do not imagine, therefore, that this has nothing to do with you, or with Jesus, just because most people categorize sickness as medical.

Now that we have such brilliant technology it is tempting to relegate all difficult and uncomfortable subjects to scientific specialists who earn money and prestige dealing with the sorts of things that seem too complicated, too disturbing, or too difficult for busy people to think about. So we can be far too ready to hand over total responsibility for our illnesses to medical professionals in the hope of staying free enough to get on with life as usual. Many people even believe scientific medical technology to be God's total provision for healing in this day and age, and consequently abrogate responsibility for all the afflictions of their own person, which is very short sighted. They follow secular advice, accept secular diagnosis and treatment, take the pills and believe that is all there is to it. They are so very trusting that they ask for treatments not only to cure their sicknesses but also to be rid of blemishes and aspects of their person that seem to be the cause of competitive disadvantage - and complain if the results are not perfect according to their own reckoning.

If we look carefully into how scientific medicine actually works, however, we discover, broadly speaking, only three different ways. Either it relieves symptoms, or it artificially corrects an apparent deficiency, or it clears the way for natural healing to occur. Thus, taking painkillers for a headache represents the simple removal of symptoms, without searching for any cause. When insulin is given for diabetes, or when thyroid tablets are given for myxoedema, or when in vitro fertilization is accepted, a major deficiency is artificially corrected. And by setting a broken limb, or by surgery for cancer, or by using antibiotics to kill infecting bacteria, a person's natural healing mechanisms can be significantly enabled. All this is clever science; but I am suggesting there is more to it than that.

We are born with healing resources living already within our own bodies. That is how God has made us. Just as skin wounds heal, given proper attention, so many other acquired conditions will often heal. Furthermore, when we come to Jesus, and are open to God's presence moving in power, major healing sometimes occurs in a very short time, which we perceive as miraculous. Therefore it behoves us to take personal responsibility for endeavouring, with God's help, to keep in good fettle our natural, God-given capacity for healing. We should endeavour to live in God's kingdom all the time and develop kingdom understanding, keeping short accounts with him. When we are sick we should come before him in the name of Jesus and claim the blessing and healing that flows from his throne. And it would help to try to understand our personal sufferings better than we do, and take more responsibility for them. We may even be willing to search diligently for meaning whenever we are ill, and bring before God, in Jesus' name, for healing, all the memories and other issues that God brings to mind at such times, including our sins and embarrassments and mistakes and difficult relationships, so that we may get rid of everything that could be getting in the way of our health and our salvation in this world. We should always be accepting of what Jesus his son did for us on the cross, and we should be listening to Holy Spirit. If in this way we endeavour to keep a healthy mind in a healthy body we shall not only become more resilient against the ubiquitous agents of death and destruction but also more open to God and better able to hear him accurately.[88]

There is no good reason for Christians to refuse to ask God to reveal the meaning of whatever suffering may come their way. There is no good reason, furthermore, why Christian spiritual healing, addressing the person as a whole rather than just the sickness in abstract, should not work alongside secular medical science when necessary.

There is no good reason for Christians to deny or put out of mind any of their experience, no matter how dreadful, and including experience of illness and suffering. And there is no good reason for them to hand their troubles in their entirety over to secular specialists. Certainly it may be necessary for secular scientists to play their part; but God actually knows about it all, and he will expect us to give him a full account of how we have responded. He will not honour unbelief, and will not excuse us just because a specialist diagnosed an illness. If we pretend otherwise we shall to some extent be living a lie. We shall be trying to exclude part of the truth of our lives from the accounting. We shall be abstracting ourselves away from certain aspects of ourselves, and we shall be living constantly with certain stresses in our souls and bodies as a result.

---

[88] Exodus 23:25-26.

Paul, in the Bible, instructs us to take captive every thought to make it obedient to Christ.[89] Thoughts come both from the present and also from the past. The past influences the present; and present experience gives rise to desires, emotions, memories, and reactions, which all come as thoughts. James the brother of Jesus tells us to confess to one another and pray for healing.[90]

Admittedly we need to be careful about what we tell other people about ourselves. God is the one who knows all the truth; he knows our very hearts. So before him we cannot in all honesty deny any of the thoughts that come into the mind. To try to put any of them out of mind in our own strength would really be a waste of effort. That way they would not be dealt with. They would stay there hidden, and may even become dangerous. Therefore it is best to admit all our thoughts to God, every one of them without censorship, and accept what Jesus did for us on the cross, and receive God's forgiveness and healing. Others who can be trusted may, of course, help us with this.

Obviously it is best to be walking with the Lord all the time, baptized in Holy Spirit, praying without ceasing, allowing God into all our thoughts constantly, and keeping short accounts with him. Surely then we would be allowing God to change the thoughts in our hearts and minds all the time. Indeed, God may then bring other related thoughts to mind, which may not always be comfortable. He may also bring new revelations about them, and new confessions, and also new hope in

---

[89] 2 Corinthians 10:5.
[90] James 5:16.

spite of the fact that it will be obvious that we cannot always be nice.

Christians may help each other to live like this; and this is the purpose of openly confessing to each other. But although Scripture encourages us to confess our sins to each other and pray for each other so that we may be healed, it also encourages us to carry our own load. That is, we are to be responsible for ourselves, and accountable as individuals to God. But we should also carry each other's burdens without becoming ill as a result.[91] This could be especially useful if we ourselves should become unwell, for surely we would be glad of disinterested truthful companionship and compassion.

To look solely to scientific technology for salvation, for a cure for every ill, therefore, is a way of avoiding being fully accountable to God. This is not to say we should not use it; rather that also we should allow God to make us aware of what else we should do and of all that appertains to our condition. The full truth of sickening experience can be hidden behind clever scientific diagnosis and remedies, and the full reality can be hidden behind abstract scientific reasoning.

Scientific method is applicable when specific outcomes are sought through practical human endeavour. It has its place. Systematic observation, classification, measurement, experiment, and the formulation, testing and modification of hypotheses, are used to create reliable technology to overcome difficulty and provide what is needed. Beyond what is needed, it can also be used to provide what is wanted. Advancing

---

[91] James 5:16 and Galatians 6:2-5.

the study of science and technology can be so very fascinating that Christians caught up in the awesome reductionism involved may easily lose sight of the place of it all in God's wider scheme of things. Even Christians may become lost in abstraction.

We have developed very extensive means for controlling our environment. As we manipulate our environment, however, we may restrict the totality of individual experience of true reality, and risk delusion. Through both manipulating our environment and also denying unpleasant aspects of ourselves we can create a place of virtual reality and live in fantasy. Creative imagination finds ways with the help of science and technology to turn fantasy into new reality, only this is an abstract reality, created by the human spirit, a sort of cushion to comfort us, an extensive transitional object that may completely enthral us. Because of what people prefer to turn a blind eye to, and because we have used our own cleverness prematurely, instead of seeking the face of God for his solutions, the reality created out of our fantastic imaginations is not God's reality. Fantasy develops when true desires seem unable to be met, in much the same way that addictions develop when we seem unable to find relief any other way. Behind both fantasy and addiction lies frustration, which, as Paul acknowledges,[92] is a condition natural to the human race. It is incumbent upon Christians to overcome their frustration, not through the flights of fantasy and manipulation but rather through seeking the face of God, laying before him their desires and feelings and

---

[92] Romans 8:20.

thoughts, and waiting with patience for his words, which will be revealed, for he promises never to leave us.[93]

If scientific method and fantasy are applied to living relationships, without taking into consideration the understanding and wisdom that come from engaging with reality fully, in truth, with God, people will be dealt with impersonally, and objectified and manipulated for the convenience of those in power. This is the danger inherent in secular nations who fail to give the Almighty God a dignified place.

You may argue that some degree of utilitarian management is necessary for government to take the broad overview necessary to be able to function efficiently. But millions have been impersonally abused, and treated as objects to be disposed of, in the wars of the last century. And people naturally object to being treated impersonally. They may be so overwhelmed and subdued as to be docile for a while, but in the long run it causes rebellion. Utilitarian management leaves out those people who do not conform to the cultural fantasy-vision, the little children, the aged, those whose spirits are weakened, the lost and confused, and the aliens, for all whom God has great compassion.

Living relationships are spiritual, and abstract laws of material, psychological and social science are not totally healing for individuals. Living beings have effects in the lives of others and in the world that cannot adequately

---

[93] Hebrews 13:5.

be quantified. Genuine love of God, of one's neighbour and of one's self can never be sceptical [94].

Certainly, therefore, it behoves any Christian professional who attends to people's needs and troubles, to meet and relate to people in a genuine and personal way, to reserve science and technology and management theory for use as appropriate, but never to neglect discernment of the spiritual influences uniquely involved. It is always necessary to bear in mind both spiritual and scientific aspects and not fall into the trap of simply applying a method or treatment to a case.

Sadly most demands of government indicate that the impersonal should be the norm, and that personal relationships, other than bland politically correct niceties, should have no place in what the state pays for. There are protocols for everything. Government insists that abstraction must be the norm for those paid by it. This way it is hoped to avoid litigation that may be sparked by differences in systems of belief and faith. In this way abstract impersonal management techniques have become effective for suppressing the challenge of Judeo-Christianity.

Military professionals, politicians and administrators, like scientists and academics, may of course be given special dispensation by us to objectify people, to disregard various aspects of human relationships, and even to kill; but they will be answerable to God for the life of others like the rest of us. Those with the living Spirit of God in them cannot afford to ignore the godly significance of every personal relationship.

----

[94] Matthew 22:37-40; 1 Timothy 6:20-21.

Abstraction

Politicians and lawyers in many countries have dictated that specifically Christian spiritual activity should have no place in the work of doctors in any practice or business that is strictly medical, because some people, particularly Humanists, Muslims and Pagans may be offended by Christianity. Christian spiritual matters are therefore to be confined to Christian religious institutions. No medical consideration is to be given to any connection there may be between an individual's soul and that individual's sickness. Indeed the very existence of the soul is doubted these days in most official quarters. Secular scientific medical technology is all the state will pay for, and all that official medical colleges will contemplate.

The rapid progress of cultural change inevitably challenges many of the preconceptions that have become set in the minds of Christians resting in the comfort of long-established Christian traditions, whose view of Christian healing may be confined to the simple offering and acceptance of prayer by accredited counsellors. But the Christian church is now quite suddenly under powerful but subtle threat throughout the world from secularism and from other religions. The preconceptions and mindsets of many Christians will need healing, and the change may not be comfortable. Christians have a choice either to live in the virtual reality of an abstract convenience-orientated society or to get real with God individually in their own spirits, souls, bodies and relationships. The issues addressed through bringing Jesus into the situation in Christian healing are not catered for by secular services.

If prayer is sought for God's healing, the person is effectively seeking both disinterested compassion and also the word of Almighty God himself which comes through the Holy Spirit. The Spirit, moreover, may use all sorts of people. It is necessary then for the supplicant to act on what the Lord personally does and says.[95] And in order not to be deceived by the world it is necessary to have the Lord's understanding of the issues involved; and in order to have his understanding it is necessary to pay careful attention to his teaching in Scripture, which does not generally accord with that of the politicians or academic institutions or even most of the churches in this world.[96] Therefore we need to pay personal attention to how God's teaching applies to the truth of our individual experience, rather than to how we were taught at school to interpret our experience. The education we have received is likely to have led us away from God's simple truth, and the religious rules we have been taught may have done so, too. It may be best simply to relate one's experience and one's suffering honestly, and to open the heart to some intelligent non-dogmatic person with Holy Spirit living in them. But even then it is essential to listen personally, oneself, to the still small voice of the real true Lord rather than to the other human being. It is necessary to be careful about seeking out righteous teaching. The wisest guidance, after committing your way to the Lord Jesus and receiving the Holy Spirit, is a rare commodity.

---

[95] James 2:14, 1 John 2:4, Micah 6:8, Deuteronomy 27:26.
[96] 1 Corinthians 1:18 – 2:16.

Certainly any church leader or elder not willing to enter into discussion with reference to the personal application of God's word, and not humble enough to reconsider his or her own opinions, must be suspect. Dogmatic prescriptions and prejudice fail to allow Holy Spirit the space and time to work through the natural resistances of a person's soul and body, and may therefore prevent personal understanding from taking root. As issues are opened up, the Holy Spirit must be allowed to be the guide in the light of holy Scripture, so that maturity and good fruit evolve. Slick and clever methods for achieving enlightenment not only quench the Spirit but also substitute demonic religion for the truth by enticing the supplicant into abstractions. Although you are saved, once you have committed your life to Jesus, that is often when trouble starts, and what God allows you to be confronted with once you belong to him is to be used by you to gain maturity. He wants you equipped for your place in his kingdom, and he has sent his Holy Spirit to be your guide.

Of course it is true that all we need do to receive healing is open our hearts to Jesus. The experience of coming into the kingdom of God, and of being accepted warts and all, is the beginning of real healing. But then an awful lot of stuff can get in the way of change and maturity. It must always be worthwhile to attempt to break strongholds of the mind through undermining lies of the devil, but it is a battle. This, nevertheless, is the path of understanding. Since it reveals the nature of sin it may be expected to be uncomfortable. But we may put our cares and reactions and sin on the cross. Jesus took it all. Holy Spirit is our comforter and encourager.

Scripture warns us against false teachers. We should beware of those who tell us what our itching ears want to hear. We should test the spirits of everyone who seeks to influence us.[97] Sometimes perforce this leads to radical and uncomfortable decisions. If healing is to be the business of Christians, unthinking acceptance of the comforts of medical and psychological science, and of the hegemony of academic teaching, particularly in the fields of theology, philosophy and politics, will have to be challenged. The seductions of false religion, even false 'Christian' religion, will also have to be avoided.

The fact is that God wants us born again, out of this unreal world and into the kingdom of heaven through accepting Jesus and receiving Holy Spirit. And he wants to equip us in our spirits, souls and bodies, through engaging with all the reality we are confronted with in this world in the light of his truth and his presence. This is real. It is not theory.

---

[97] 2 John 7 and 1 John 4:1.

Chapter 6 - The Spirit of Greece

By the grace of God I have had the freedom to think outside the secular humanistic Greek box during most of my working life. I doubt whether younger doctors could earn their living now if they were to apply the sort of deliberations the Lord has led me into. There are many more political sanctions than there used to be against specifically Christian interpretations of professional experience. The medical community exclude anyone who dares to make any basic paradigm shift in their thinking away from secular scientific humanism. Real spiritual involvement in the actual healing of people with classified medical disorders is not something doctors are actually permitted to involve themselves with. Cure is dependent on scientifically regulated evidence. Cure, nevertheless, differs from healing.

That is why I believe God wants His kingdom people immediately involved in healing ministry, both with each other and with others who seek Jesus in their suffering. And I believe that for this to occur his kingdom people must think in a Hebraic way rather than in a secular or classical Greek way.

We can leave scientific biomedicine to the specialists. It has its place. But it can be complemented by God's kingdom people who think in a Hebraic manner, outside the confines of that secular box, and empowered by Holy Spirit. Believe me, it is time for this!

Other people of other religions are realising that ethnocentric world views (as they say) may help people give greater meaning to their sicknesses and sufferings, and thus assist the acceptance of medical technology and assist healing. Very reasonable non-Christian books are written about this. So it is time for Christian spiritual healing to be reckoned with. And, for this to happen, it is necessary for the church to think like disciples of Jesus. I believe the Holy Spirit wants me to say: "Do not be afraid to be different. Those who turn to Jesus for healing should apply Hebraic understanding. Apply it radically to the roots of your sicknesses. Expect miracles. But remember there is no need for conflict with scientific medicine, for the two can work together."

Scientific medicine is necessary these days for most disease; but Christian spiritual healing complements it. The church can work alongside the medical scientists for those who want deeper healing. Science can apply the first aid and the splint; but it is in the name of Jesus that the root cause can be eradicated and the person healed.

In order to minister spiritual healing in the name of Jesus it is necessary to overcome secular thinking with Jesus' understanding. And this implies some understanding in Hebraic terms. After all, Scripture says, "And all thy children shall be taught of the Lord" (Isaiah 54:13 and John 6:45). And the hand of God has always been on His people. God developed godly understanding within Jewish culture, using Hebrew concepts and Hebrew language as used in Scripture, for twenty centuries and more before the time of Jesus. But, because the Holy Spirit was not experienced as being so active with them as He has been since Jesus ascended into heaven, the understanding before the time of Jesus was more limited than that of the earliest Christians. Occasional healings by the power of the Holy Spirit are recorded in the Old Testament, but Jesus went about healing the sick all the time. All who came to Him were healed. He healed fever, skin disease, paralysis, deformity, blindness, deafness, muteness, epilepsy, bleeding, even death, and He delivered people from demons. He made no analysis of why people were sick, apart from implying a general connection with sin. We should be aware, however, that He lived and moved in a culture in which people spoke about themselves and their relationships in a very direct way, without abstract theory (unlike us). Their understanding about themselves and their relationships and sicknesses was as recorded in the Old Testament; and it was different from ours today. The connection of sickness with sin was inherent in the Hebrew culture at the time of Jesus, as is apparent from the taunt to the man born blind, whom Jesus healed, "You were steeped in sin at birth..." (John 9:34). And I am suggesting that if we listen to the guidance of the Holy Spirit, and pay careful attention to Scripture, it is nowhere near so difficult as we may imagine to develop that same sort of Hebraic understanding for ourselves now. In fact I believe it is God's will that we should do so. And I believe that in these end times He will send more of His supernatural power to break through again, like they saw when Jesus was walking on this earth two thousand years ago.

Although Jesus had given power and authority to His disciples to drive out all demons and to heal every disease and sickness (Matthew 10:1, Luke 9:1), and had instructed them to make disciples of all nations, and baptise them, and teach them to do all that Jesus had taught His disciples to do (Matthew 28:20), the ministry of healing seems quite rapidly to have died down after the time of Jesus. There is not much mention of it for hundreds of years, apart from occasional miracles, until the Pentecostal revivals of the past century.

Jerusalem was destroyed in 70 AD, and again in 135, and Hebrew culture was scattered. Christians distanced themselves from Jews, and Jews from Christians. And Greek ways of understanding, that had been developing for five hundred years, under the guidance of brilliant pagan philosophers such as Socrates, Plato and Aristotle, increasingly preponderated in a world now also inhabited by Christians. Early church fathers such as Irenaeus, Tertullian, Origen, Jerome, and Augustine, all contended with Greek thinking and mostly failed to avoid being subtly, but nevertheless profoundly, influenced by it. Then in the thirteenth century Thomas Aquinas integrated Aristotle into Christian orthodoxy. So, with the Renaissance, Greece triumphed again. Petrarch and Erasmus, notably overcame the scholasticism of moribund institutional Roman religion. Eventually Greek humanism allied with Christianity bestowed upon us the Enlightenment, bringing the expectation that the world can be made better by human effort. Thus the influence of classical Greek thinking can be seen to have prevailed in the church up to the present day. It is particularly to be found in the extent of the unbelief that disconnects religious ritual observance from everyday living. Jesus promised real abundant life. For two thousand years the spirit of Greece has seriously distorted the application and celebration of the gospel.

Of course, Greek thinking assisted the efficient administration of conquest, domination and trade in the Western world, from the time of the Roman Empire more or less to the present day. And for hundreds of years rulers bent on conquest have succeeded in controlling populations and organising them for their advantage. To describe the process succinctly, from a Christian perspective, let it suffice to say that instead of being guided by prophetic revelation and the word of God, governments have employed administrators to analyse and classify situations systematically into abstract concepts, and then to apply humanistic theory in order to manipulate for political advantage. This is the classical Greek way. And many Christians have innocently been caught up in it, having been employed for their trustworthiness and their biddable, moral and proficient natures, which were of great assistance for controlling and containing unruly people. Colluding with administrators in the face of overwhelming problems, many of these Christians forgot the salvation available in the kingdom of God.

One consequence of the distortion of the gospel by humanistic Greek thinking was that large numbers of seriously traumatised people thrown off from the Crusades, between the eleventh and thirteenth centuries, and later from the Hundred Years' War in Europe, between the fourteenth and fifteenth centuries, received little or no help for healing, although monasteries would sometimes give them shelter. Traumatised, both physically and spiritually wounded, separated from their families, deceived and tormented, they were goaded into ships and cast adrift, or herded into old deserted leper hospitals. Sometimes they were given alms as they wandered about, but only very rarely were they met with compassion, or with any godly understanding of the nature and extent of their suffering. Nor were they prayed with in the name of the Lord Jesus with faith for deliverance and healing as the Bible commands. Those were the days in which people first sang "Hark, Hark! The dogs do bark, The beggars are coming to town, Some in rags and some in tags and one in a velvet gown..."

Much later, when there were large numbers of displaced people crowding into cities from the countryside to try to find new factory work during the Industrial Revolution, distresses and diseases began to be understood scientifically in an abstract way, and classified, in order to allocate resources for managing sickness, madness, vagrancy and criminality in hospitals and asylums and workhouses and prisons. The main priority became management of distress. Practical assistance was given to alleviate suffering by those charitably inclined. But compassionate and detailed personal prayer for healing was almost unheard of. Although they may occasionally have received some kindness, most people just had to grin and bear it.

Until the days of Florence Nightingale there was little understanding of how the process of healing could be assisted by care. At the time of the First World War some soldiers were shot for having developed severe combat stress. And only since the end of the Second World War have we had antibiotics to help with infections. Only in the past hundred years or so has the discipline of psychotherapy made it socially acceptable to listen to people's distress and search for understanding.

A dearth of hope caused the true nature and effect of a vast amount of deception, pain and suffering to go unrecorded. There is so much that has not been able to be talked about. Our ancestors were accustomed to much more everyday horror, distress and pain than we are. Until fairly recently, little or no space and time was ever given for the development of understanding sufficiently profound to give truly credible meaning to personal suffering so that healing might be facilitated.

Some Christians shy away from the very idea of such understanding, believing the past should be put behind us and forgotten by effort of will. But in practice the past does not get forgotten, despite efforts of will, because without forgiveness and healing the wounds of the past remain active, and they influence behaviour.

The reason for true godly understanding is to avoid misunderstanding. Events and reactions to events have to come to light and be spoken about before God, and they often need to be remembered painfully in order to be forgiven and healed. This is repentance. Although every belief system under the sun has its own understanding and rationality, including humanistic psychological science, I believe it is only truly safe to come out with sensitive memories, thoughts and feelings, under the active spiritual authority of the Lord Jesus Christ, because only then can truth come to light and be reconciled to God and completely healed. Only then do we not, in fact, rely on our own understanding. And in all our ways we actually acknowledge Him, as it says in Proverbs 3:5-6.

So from the European so-called Enlightenment of the seventeenth and eighteenth centuries there came new methods of investigation. New facts were discovered, systematically studied, classified and abstractly speculated upon. New hypotheses were developed and experimented upon. New machines and technologies were developed. And also new systems of control, administration and management were put into effect to make it easier to obtain economic advantage in trade, and to facilitate government. Since then, science has continued to evolve to an astonishing extent, and has transformed the practicalities of life so that today our many conveniences and technologies quite commonly give us what we want at the touch of a button, and it has become hard to cope without them.

It has become compellingly fashionable, furthermore, to believe methods of scientific enquiry to have superseded all other reasoning. The only knowledge worth having is factual. Knowing a person, loving and respecting a person, and being influenced by a person, is not as significant as having the facts to make 'right' choices. Wisdom is doubted unless outcomes can be measured. The sceptical spirit of secular scientific humanism today makes people believe that it lies within their human powers to solve the ills of the world without any reference to God. So profoundly is this now the case that almost no Christian ever seems open to wonder that these days we might actually have more faith in our science than in our God.

Since the Second World War medical technology has burgeoned to provide an enormous variety of drugs and methods to suppress symptoms of suffering. This very technology is the product of systematic academic scientific reasoning, confirmed by experiment and trial. The medical drugs and machines and buildings are manufactured using large quantities of capital deployed to keep everyone happy as much as reasonably possible whilst we strive for further progress to control of our environment.

Biblical enquiry into root causes of misery has been avoided for two thousand years. It has always been far too uncomfortable to consider the perverse nature of mankind. Nowadays it would even be politically incorrect, and any manifest discomfort would be scientifically diagnosed and treated with drugs, rather than truly understood.

Suddenly, however, we are faced with two big problems that this humanistic scientific system has brought upon itself: 1) the money is running out; and 2) people will no longer be tolerant of a forced return to poverty, disease, discomfort and insecurity. Across the world people have become dependent on science and state provision to enable them to seem to fare increasingly well as 'continuous improvement' evolves.

Therefore it is necessary to ask two personal questions. Let us be honest! (1) Do you in truth put all your faith in biomedicine and the National Health Service when you are ill? (2) Do you seek the Lord for what He might be saying to you regarding the root cause of your sickness?

A large number of Christians assume that medical science is the gift of God for healing. For a long time now it has been tacitly assumed that medical technology is a gift from God for the healing of the nations. Medical aid exported by missionaries may even seem sometimes to have greater priority than the gospel. When they are ill, Christian people just seem to trust the doctors to do all that is necessary. Although they may get the church to pray for them, there is commonly a lack of the understanding necessary for hearing what the Lord might be saying to them personally. They are not attuned to the Lord's wavelength, as it were. Their minds are actually more closed than they assume because they do not think Hebraically. Their minds do not work the same way that Jesus' mind, and the minds of His hearers, did two thousand years ago. I think the reason for this may be related to a reluctance to be familiar with the Old Testament. It really requires a paradigm shift of thinking, although one that should not be too difficult for those who know Jesus as Lord and have Holy Spirit living in them. We should not forget that the Old Testament was Jesus' Bible.

According to my reading of the whole Bible, the causes of sickness relate to the fallen state of humanity; in other words, to sin. Leviticus 26 and Deuteronomy 28 are utterly relevant. I believe this was essentially assumed to be the case in the culture in which Jesus lived. And I am saying that the classical Greek humanistic mindset of our present-day culture makes it necessary for Christians, when they are ill, to adjust their thinking when they seek the Lord for healing. And it is necessary for them to involve themselves in personal repentance, under the guidance of Holy Spirit, if the root causes are to be dealt with. There was no need for people to be taught this in Jerusalem two thousand years ago, because everyone generally presumed it to be the case; but it is necessary to proceed in this way everywhere in the world now.

We live in a culture, moreover, in which many people complain that medical treatment is impersonal. Increasingly it is a cause of dissatisfaction that all you seem to get is the technology. And it is a fact that the government will not pay for time spent in professional personal relationship which may unearth deeper issues. In a multi-faith society this is understandable because, since the results cannot be unequivocally measured, what is being paid for cannot be controlled. Since our British nation has lost its Christian identity, secular scientific medical personnel no longer even consider that any personal meaning attached to an illness might be of significance. The Buddhists and the Hindus and the pagans, however, some of them academically very respectable (and we should note that the first academy was founded by Plato in pagan classical Greece) are very interested to offer a listening ear and to proselytize by giving meaning to sufferings according to their various spiritual systems.

As technological medicine is found to be inadequate, more and more people may nevertheless be willing to turn to the Lord Jesus. After all, He is the only one to offer complete healing without deception. Therefore it is necessary for Christians to allow themselves to be equipped to meet the need in these end times.

Essentially, the Greek way of thinking that has so powerfully prevailed in Western civilisation, and spread throughout the world, does not recognise mankind as made in the image of God. Nor does it allow for man to call on the Creator and King of the Universe, and for Him to answer in such a way as to save people.

According to the spirit of Greece, all enquiry into human nature and our relationships with the world we inhabit is made without including God. Therefore there is an inherent sense of not being sure, and therefore of needing proof. We extensively use our five senses, and measurement, and our systematic scientific reasoning, but ignore the intuition that can come from the one true God. Evidence from the senses is doubted because so often it proves unreliable. Measurement and systematic reasoning are used in addition to achieve greater certainty. According to classical Greek thought, reality can be known by the mind, but revelation comes from diverse sources. Mind was separate from body, and spirit was separate from matter. The soul had an immortal, divine part, the seat of personality, to which the mind had access, but it also had a corrupt mortal part, which included desire, which always interfered to create uncertainty. And since error was always possible much debate was necessary. Methods of discussion were evolved to try to eliminate error both human and divine. And resultant hypotheses were tested. To this day these sceptical Greek ways of thinking are found in all academic institutions. Speculations give rise to hypotheses which are tested, and systematic classifications are developed with the same abstract theorising. Academic institutions in the classical Greek tradition have become the arbiters of truth and falsehood, and of right and wrong in our parliament and in our courts of law.

Yet there must always be a question, amongst the recipients of the results of this Greek sort of thinking, about whether or not the perceptions upon which the results are based are valid. Different facets of experience may be considered as evidence but they may not be complete. Some aspects may remain disconnected, some may be dissociated, and some not fully thought through. The spiritual power that enabled available knowledge to be used to really powerful effect was mysterious to the Greeks. And consequently their scepticism has always been influenced by demonic principalities and powers. Despite their brilliance, they did not know the Lord Jesus.

Greek concepts of freedom and happiness depend upon making right choices, which depends upon factual knowledge; Aristotle said it also depends upon personal character. According to this way of thinking, if a person knows what is right, he can do it. We see the modern influence of this thinking in educational theory that assumes intelligence to be the ability to make right choices, and assumes that pupils will be able to do what they are taught.

Eight hundred years ago the philosopher Duns Scotus challenged these assumptions, which were implicit in the writings of his contemporary Thomas Aquinas, who, as mentioned previously, had recently squared Christianity with Aristotle. Duns Scotus said a person's will was more powerful than a person's intellect, and he thus acknowledged that a person's will could be under spiritual direction, which could powerfully influence what was learned. But the supporters of Aquinas prevailed, and they have continued to do so for the past eight hundred years. They even mockingly arranged for supporters of Duns Scotus to be called "dunces" after his first name, just to rub salt into the wound when they did not do as they were told. Paul speaks of this in Romans Chapter 7, where it is made quite clear that Duns Scotus was right.

In vivid contrast, the Hebrew spirit is direct, alive and emotional. The Hebrew instinctively connects thought with the body, plainly saying how it is. They know in that culture when their perception is substantive, and they have a greater certainty in knowing. The individual is seen as a whole. Spirit, soul and body are not separate. The seat of the personality is the living body.

A potential unity is automatically assumed to exist between any part and the whole; and God, to whom each individual is answerable, is the person who holds the whole together, whether they know it or not, because God has had his hand in their lives for several millennia. Guided by the hand of God through the patriarchs and prophets, and by the word of God, Hebrew culture has little interest in speculative thinking or theories except for practical purposes. Science is useful, of course, and they use it well. But abundant living can never be reduced to scientific expediency.

Freedom, for the Hebrew, actually comes from being right with God. A person is how he ought to be when he obeys the maker's instructions. Such righteousness, however, is impossible without God's living Holy Spirit, without loving God. Holy Spirit begets obedience. And he comes to live in you when you really personally accept redemption by Jesus' blood and his sacrifice and victory on the cross.

In the New Testament letters of Paul, and of John, we find particular warnings about the classical Greek way of abstract spiritualizing, or theorizing, about what is lived out for real in the flesh (e.g. 1 Corinthians 1:18-25, 1 John 4:1-3, 2 John 7, Revelation 2:6 & 15). In 1 Timothy 5:20 (KJV) Paul warns about "the oppositions of science falsely so called". In the New International Version Paul's sentence reads, "Turn away from godless chatter and the opposing ideas of what is falsely called knowledge", which philosophers today may recognise as a reference to equipollence, a Greek method, still commonly used, of setting equally strong propositions into opposition, leading to suspension of judgement, denial of any guilt or conscience, abstract reasoning, political compromises, and the alleged tranquillity of absence of belief, which they called 'epoche'.

This sort of classical Greek academic philosophy has profoundly influenced Christian belief and practice from the earliest days of Christianity to the present day by disconnecting it from the Holy Spirit and godly reality. Thus the spirit of Greece has subtly changed the Hebraic teachings of our Lord Jesus and caused various aspects to be put out of our minds. Unknowingly we have become accustomed to thinking in many respects like pagan classical Greeks.

Whether or not we can ever be right before God if we attempt to understand the Old and New Testaments in a Greek way must therefore be questionable. It seems incumbent upon Christians to repent of having allowed the spirit of classical Greece to close their ears and eyes and hearts. Our Bibles were intended by God to be read in Holy Spirit so as to allow the presence of the Lord to change our understanding, to reconnect us both with ourselves and also with him, and to make our understanding like his understanding. This is the way for ancient wells of living water to be re-opened (Galatians 3:14, Isaiah 12:3).

We should take careful note of Daniel's dream of the ram and the goat (recorded in Chapter 8) and accept the prophecy that out of this principality of classical Greece, which is now growing increasingly powerful amongst us as rebels grow completely wicked, there will arise a master of intrigue who will become very strong, and throw truth to the ground and deceive many, bringing destruction and desolation. "Yet he will be destroyed, but not by human power." (Daniel 8:25).

Zechariah 9:13 says, "I will rouse your sons, O Zion, against your sons, O Greece, and make you like a warrior's sword."

Chapter 7 – Philosophical Sketch

"I buy a paper, glance at the headlines, check the lottery, skim over the sports page, jump on the bus and find a seat. A spaced out young woman comes to sit down next to me in a world of her own, muttering to herself, and she irritates and embarrasses me. I keep myself to myself and gaze out of the window, watching the congested traffic. Everyone seems stressed. The bus stops and starts through the rush hour. I worry about our mortgage, about paying for our holiday, about keeping my job, about my little daughter's visit to the doctor this morning with an ear infection. It begins to pour with rain. At the roundabout, I jump off the bus as usual and jog the two hundred yards to the office. Jim says, "Hi, mate, you're late." I grunt, sit at my desk, start the computer, open the emails, and begin my replies. I have not thought for a moment about all this stuff since I left work yesterday, but now it all comes crashing back. Frequently I have to check myself to avoid offending the people I am writing to.

"About eleven o'clock, I pay for a plastic mug of strong superhot coffee from the machine in the corridor. Cynthia gets one, too, and smiles at me. So I ask if she'd had a good time last night, because she was going to see a film with her bloke. She said it was boring. I smile and saunter back to my work. She'll soon be finding another man, no doubt. At lunchtime I bump into Mike at the sandwich bar. We spend a pleasant half hour dissecting the latest football. We go to support the same team every Saturday.

"In the afternoon I take a pool car and visit one of our projects in another part of town, spending an hour negotiating details and checking for mistakes and problems. All the time I make notes assessing costs. Back at the office I file a detailed report, then spend the remaining half hour trying again to catch up on more of my backlog of complex internet correspondence.

"Back home late, I kiss my weary wife and look her in the eyes with sincere appreciation. She finished her job before me and is busy now cooking supper. After we have all eaten I try to show some interest in the children's homework. My wife goes off to her yoga class. I settle down soon with a beer in front of the television to watch a favourite soap. Later I join the kids in a computer game before they go to bed. My wife and I are soon in bed ourselves. We exchange snippets of conversation about events at work, the children's schooling, the doctor's treatment, her friends at the class, the shopping we'll do on Sunday, money and the mortgage, and the practical matters that clutter our lives. We are both very tired. We fall soundly asleep. Next day it all starts again."

Many people could give a similar sort of mundane account of their day. And although personal and topical embellishments could be added, they would probably be no more inspired, no more imaginative or reflective. They would all have worries, and owe, and get ill. Despite all their endeavours and stressful concerns, however, let us note that everything is more or less taken care of. Even if they can no longer keep on working there will be support from the state to help them manage somehow. Although much of the day will have become habitual, we may observe that much is taken for granted. The doctor treats illness. The children attend school. Food comes from the supermarket. Television and computers provide entertainment. Through sophisticated organization of communication, social welfare and education, and through complex science and technology, the culture and environment are trusted to be fairly constant. Politicians adjust legal controls in the hope that undue strife may be avoided. Whatever sort of inadvertent slavery individuals may be trapped in goes largely unacknowledged. There is no time for thoughts about that sort of thing - such deep issues are far too threatening. It seems best for people to remain habitually content, routinely occupied and accustomed to regular everyday stresses.

The detailed knowledge to sustain this sort of regular existence, (the knowledge necessary for taking the bus, reading the paper, managing relationships, using the computer, calculating costs and doing business, answering letters, being father or mother in a family, doing the shopping, cooking, washing, cleaning, mending, studying, watching football, and so on) will have been acquired through experiences growing up, imitating and understanding others, making sense of reading, allowing oneself to be taught in the family, and at work, school and college, and forming habits. We shall have been taught to make sense of experience through sufficient reasoning, according to customary cultural sense and private choice. If we think about it, each one of us will have to acknowledge that, through the business of growing up with other people, many various formative experiences will have been assimilated automatically, and unquestioningly used as examples, from which we have developed our own individual responses to new events that have personally confronted us. In this way we have developed our own individual character, and grown in maturity so as to be able to find our place in society. Later our minds will have been further informed and safeguarded by systems of thought and practice constantly developing within us through our reason and imagination, with inspiration from a multitude of people and sources, including spiritual influences. The culture and parental environment we have been brought up in will have influenced us profoundly, and much of this will have been taken for granted.

The civilization of England was powerfully influenced, from the Middle Ages onwards, by the institution of nominally Christian churches, mostly housed in imposing buildings, and by schools and universities in which Christian values were commonly accepted as the norm until the late twentieth century. The prestige of the established church was guaranteed by being of service to government as a pillar of stability. A dignified place in national life was given to it and, in tacit recognition that the spiritual power of the Christian gospel could be disturbing, senior church appointments were politically controlled, with the monarch as its titular head. This system generally assisted the overcoming of national enemies, helped trade to flourish, brought justice into law, and curtailed hardship and suffering particularly through imaginative developments in science and technology. Since the later twentieth century, however, mainstream Christian influence has been almost lost. The two World Wars were followed by rebellion against the old order, which seemed eventually to have let everyone down. There has been a consequent influx of other, alternative, powerful spiritual influences, both from Eastern nations and from ancient Western paganism.. The dividends of centuries of Christian stability are still being reaped by those who have a regular job and can pay the mortgage, such as the man whose day was just briefly described; but greater instability seems to threaten.

Under the tolerant covering of established Christianity there was much national blessing. Two other different spiritual systems, however, had found it possible to develop their influence within it from the earliest days. The philosophy and paganism of Classical Greece established themselves as parasites in Christian institutions, and have gradually weakened their hosts for two millennia. The learning of classical Greece, with its pagan gods and its idealistic humanism, was preserved by Islam in the Middle East and in Spain, and was welcomed in the Middle Ages by European scholars and universities. Salient details were adopted for the evolution of science. The process of scientific evolution was gradual at first, but slowly it gathered momentum, as more and more practical advantages became apparent. A first spectacular flowering occurred with the Italian Renaissance of Greek and Roman learning, which spread throughout Europe. The romanticism of all that gave way to profound practical changes in the lives of everyone as the European Enlightenment took hold. Thereafter the complexity and usefulness of science and technology have grown exponentially. Following the First World War demand for a better world harnessed all sorts of new technologies for modernisation. Now we have eventually reached a time when the obvious benefits of the drive for continuous improvement have caused many people to question the relevance of Judeo-Christian faith. Postmodern culture encourages people to do what they want, believe what they want and think what they want, assuming all values are relative to what feels to be good for the majority. Man is the measure of all things, as the classical Greeks said. Loving your neighbour as yourself may be a popular socialist ideal, but loving the Lord God our Father is commonly mocked and even hated. There is increasing opposition to the purposes of God, with respect to personal holiness and the place of Israel, as described in the Bible. Fallen human nature is, in fact, full of envy for the ideals of the God of life, whom they deny; yet those who hold to the promises of God are seen as hypocrites because their apologetics no longer seem credible.

Classical scholarship has been taught in most places of higher education for centuries. It has made the study of ancient Greek mythology so respectable that it has long been a substitute for Christianity amongst nominal Christians in polite society. The exclamation "By Jove!" was commonly used until very recently to signify something similar to "By Jehovah!" or to "By God!" although Jove was the Roman god Jupiter, who was the same as the Greek god Zeus. Belief in the actual existence of the pagan gods of ancient Greece is indeed half serious, for it has allowed people to think that maybe various gods with real spiritual powers do indeed have some influence over what happens in this world, although they cannot be sure, and certainly would never commit themselves. Those few individuals who have actually committed themselves wholeheartedly to pagan deities (some of whom have a profound personal knowledge of pagan spirituality that we should take very seriously indeed) have for a long time, however, been able to flourish and wield occult influence behind the scenes in this humanist-Christian culture. Members of the exclusive eighteenth century Hell Fire Club were a classic example. And they have borne abundant fruit. There are many more modern examples.

Institutional churches adapted their theology accordingly, by compromise, most notably with the help of Thomas Aquinas (1225-74) who had made the teaching of the classical Greek Aristotle acceptable to the Pope. Aquinas' theology was intellectual, based in objective reasoning. He failed to give sufficient recognition to the personal effects of spiritual power arguing, despite 1 Corinthians Chapter 2, that people cannot have direct knowledge of God. He considered intellect more powerful than the will, failing to recognize the effect on the will of spiritual commitment. His practical philosophy suited a world in which human beings, constantly troubled by the exigencies of war, were becoming very clever at building and making things, and consequently profiting from trade. His influence, in effect, assisted humanist power and ingenuity to be given ecclesiastical permission to build a world as perfect as practically possible for the prosperity of Christendom, on condition that they obey ecclesiastical rules. Objective humanistic reasoning and latent paganism, combined with fallen human nature, influenced the widespread development of church traditions that distorted true interpretation of Scripture and quenched the Spirit. The power and authority of the Holy Spirit have been increasingly on the wane in institutional churches because an increasing proportion of Christians have been effectively living as enemies of the cross of Christ, with their mind on earthly things.[98] Paganism and humanism have not been sufficiently visible and therefore have not been challenged. The inevitable sclerosis has now set in.[99]

Less noticeably, however, and with the sacrifice of many saints' lives, the person of the Lord Jesus Christ was revealed as personal redeemer and saviour to a small but increasing number of individuals, most particularly through the translation of Scripture into everyday language, which went on quietly throughout the centuries amongst groups of genuine Christians. The true kingdom of God has been growing in consequence

---

[98] Philippians 3:17-4:1.
[99] 2 Thessalonians 2:6-12.

all over the world for two thousand years, both in numbers and in wisdom.[100]

Yet now, in the first part of the twenty-first century after Messiah, England has shed Christian allegiance and become forcefully secular, which of course is an euphemism for pagan. Responding to the prevailing climate, politicians have made laws that ignore Biblical wisdom. Quite suddenly it is politically correct to believe God to be an anachronism. After industrialization and imperialism had brought misery to millions, and after two world wars wreaked the most appalling devastation and carnage, people have asked why God, if he exists, has allowed such terrible, dreadful events to occur.

Institutional churches and academic theologians have eventually confounded the understanding of the word of God in the Holy Bible to such an extent that people are blind both to the justice of God and also to the inadequacies of legalism. The possibility of genuine heartfelt repentance, healing and change is being denied to many people in consequence. Since they have lost the fear of God, the hope and joy that come from accepting God's only begotten son and allowing Holy Spirit to sanctify the whole person is portrayed rather feebly as an exhilarating lifestyle choice. In effect many churches have looked in earnest to other religions, and are full of secular humanism. Many even believe all religions worship the same god. Accepting without question all the apparent benefits of investment in science, and the

---

[100] A record may be found in E.H. Broadbent (1931) *"The Pilgrim Church."*

pleasing logic of academics, and the effectiveness of media psychology and of fiat money, they effectively put their faith in the ingenuity of mankind to control their environment. Many of their members actually look to mysticism, superstition, prescription drugs and seductive entertainment as legitimate lifestyle choices for relief of stress. They do not realise that their theology has essentially reverted to that of pagan classical Greece.

Those with discernment, however, can see the hypocrisy; so it should be no surprise to them to find an accompanying resurgence of the ancient paganism of the land that was suppressed for a while by the ascendancy, diplomacy and occasional spiritual fervour of the Christian church centuries ago.

*

The classical Greek philosopher Plato (who lived about 427-347 BC) had argued that the capacity for learning and understanding what is good and right lies innate within the soul of each person, and waits to be divinely enlightened, through the discipline of philosophy, to the truth of being. The human mind already knew how to live, he said, but needed philosophical enlightenment in order to function freely. Knowledge was divinely theoretical, and not to be confused with experience or perception. The mind was separate from the body because truth and certainty could not be discovered through physical experience. Sensation, with associated feelings and memories, and with an infinite variety of personal perceptions, implications, emotions and interpretations, could not be trusted. The origin of actual truth must be divine; and it seemed to be accessible through abstract reasoning. Most people were not sophisticated enough to use such divine reason for common benefit. Therefore the family was not to be trusted with the guidance and instruction of children.[101] Every family was to be subordinate to the state, which was to be ruled by the enlightened. It was the state that was to be believed in and trusted rather than the parents. Plato therefore advocated that people should be carefully instructed and managed, because there were not many who were able to achieve sufficient philosophical enlightenment to rule. And he said that those people with the best natures had a duty to accept public office so as to guide and educate others.[102]

Plato's philosophy has been enormously influential, and remains relevant to this day because there are many people in all political parties, academic institutions and churches who seriously consider this to be the only way to organize society. His thinking underpins the imposition of secular state values (political correctness) rather than encouragement of individual accountability before God; it also underlies the modern fashion for changing the interpretation of tried and tested laws and morals that were based in Christian ethics; it informs the distrust of people rather than policy, and the derogation of fathers; and the drive for continuous change by way of "improvement" driven by science and financial profit; and the imposition of national curricula for education;

---

[101] Many British public schools have espoused the same philosophy.

[102] Plato: "*Republic*," Book VII.

and the belief that there is nothing to be trusted but the logic of what is academically deduced and democratically acceptable; and the celebration of unity in diversity (which in truth celebrates the mixture of good with evil); and the belief that human beings are essentially good; and Christian universalism, and so on. It is also behind designs for one world government and a new world order, and the massive contemporary challenge to biblical Christianity.

Thus it may be seen that the modern day described at the beginning of this chapter is democratically controlled by these secular values, in denial of the one true God. Although almighty God has had a profound influence on our culture for eighty generations, and has brought substantial political stability, particularly through the established church, the place of the Christian God is now being denied to him. It should therefore be noted with grave concern that his blessings have been forfeited. The nation that once was Christian has come under his judgement for not keeping faith with him. The word of God to our nation is, "Return to me and I will return to you."[103]

Without him, the harnessing of secular democracy to the pursuit of profit through science creates an environment controlled through human ingenuity and all sorts of false gods. Politicians unfettered from Scriptural authority now have power to make laws for their benefit, to control access to information, and to manipulate how people think using media technology and psychological science. Unless the God of Israel is

---

[103] Zechariah 1:3; Malachi 3:7.

given a dignified place and significant influence, not only in the state but also in what people see and hear and are exposed to, we shall lapse very easily into totalitarianism. And although totalitarianism can sometimes seem benign, there can never be any guarantee that it will always be so. When the unexpected happens, earthquake, epidemic, famine, revolution, war, financial disaster, and death, the comforts provided by science, humanistic academic thinking and secular politics may be found wanting. Who then will people turn to?

Sixteen hundred years or so after Plato, there developed in Europe, amongst scholars and thinking people, a time of cultural excitement about the rediscovery of ancient knowledge from classical Greek and Roman manuscripts, many of which had been preserved in Islamic libraries. Roger Bacon (1214 – 1294) an academic at the then newly established University of Oxford made a statement that concisely describes a significant shift in thinking that was powerfully moving people away from the old scholastic dogma that had been used by institutional churches to instruct people in nominal Christianity. The need for actual personal experience in order to be certain of facts seems to have been gleaned from newly discovered writings of Aristotle, who was Plato's successor. Instead of allowing the person of Jesus to lead them by his Spirit into all truth, however, they exulted in what they could do, in their own strength, with things. Roger Bacon wrote that he "...now wishes to unfold the principles of mathematical science, since without experience nothing can be sufficiently known. For there are two modes of acquiring knowledge; namely by reasoning and experience. Reasoning draws a conclusion and makes us grant the conclusion, but does not make the conclusion certain, nor does it remove doubt so that the mind may rest on the intuition of truth, unless the mind discovers it by the method of experience; for many have the arguments relating to what can be known, but because they lack experience they neglect the arguments, and neither avoid what is harmful nor follow what is good. For if a man who has never seen fire should prove by adequate reason that fire burns and injures things and destroys them, his mind would not be satisfied thereby, nor would he avoid fire, until he placed his hand or some combustible substance in the fire, so that he might prove by experience that which reasoning taught. But when he has had actual experience of combustion his mind is made certain and rests in the full light of truth. ...And if we turn our attention to the experiences that are particular and complete and certified, or wholly in their own discipline, it is necessary to go by way of the principles of this science which is called experimental."[104]

So, according to Bacon, the full light of truth becomes apparent through human reason and human experience. Thus the practical, experimental, mathematical method of 'divinely theoretical' objective science took hold and began to be used by creative people to make things and use them for human advantage. At first its momentum developed in simple ways; but from that time onwards

---

[104] Roger Bacon: "*Opus Majus*," Part VI, translated by Robert Belle Burke for the University of Pennsylvania Press, 1928.

to this very day attempts to achieve certain knowledge and certain ends by scientific methodology have been progressing all over the world. First its influence was seen in developments of old traditions of masonry, most notably in Gothic architecture, also in armaments and military machines, and in agriculture. Artisans thought in terms of measurement, mathematics and material production. Artists perceived a new perspective, less idiomatic, more mathematical – one of the first seems to have been Giotto. Goods were made in greater abundance, trade increased and the population grew. And now, a thousand or so years later, the lives of millions all over the world depend upon scientific achievements.

The medieval Roman church was seriously threatened by the new learning. It seemed liable to lose control of people's beliefs. Despite all its conclaves and councils, its understanding of Scripture had become so sclerotic that it could not see the new approach to learning in the light of divine revelation, in order to deal rightly with all the implications according to the word of God. The perceived threats were resisted by force. The Pope reacted by authorising crusades to halt the advance of Islam. And he set up the Inquisition to eradicate heresy from Christendom.

As useful things were made, trade increased, and populations grew throughout the world. Change and trouble multiplied cruelty and wickedness. The English waged wars for hegemony with Scotland and with France. Throughout Europe monarchs fought for power and trade. From the north and east Christendom was threatened by pagans and Ottomans. There was fighting everywhere, anarchy and terrible brutality. Many people were displaced, and thousands of tormented souls and destitute wanderers made communities restless and hopeless. Leprosy and other diseases were imported from the east. Then in the middle of the thirteen hundreds there came plague, killing millions throughout Europe.

Amongst newly discovered manuscripts were found Greek and Hebrew copies of Scripture that were used by Wyclif, at Oxford, to translate the Bible into English. Rather suddenly, as a result, the word of God was heard and read directly by lay people, bypassing the clergy, who had hitherto controlled knowledge of Scripture by making sure they were the sole interpreters of the Latin Vulgate. Wyclif sent out preachers to interpret the gospel in plain biblical terms. Serious spiritual questions were widely raised, in consequence, about the authority hitherto assumed by the institutional church. Simple, ignorant, distressed people woke up to the blatant hypocrisy and wickedness found everywhere, and they reacted with despair, and sometimes with violence. Commonly they failed to understand enough of Jesus' teaching to keep the peace. In England at this time circumstances were not helped by the imposition of a Poll Tax. English Peasants revolted in 1381 and the Revolt was put down with duplicity and severity by King Richard II. Thereafter the social structure of England changed. Kings and barons fought for power and advantage. Advances were made in the use of gunpowder and armaments. But the manorial system, with its serfdom, was broken. People became freer to develop their own business. Sheep farming expanded due to the demand throughout Europe for cloth. As the wool trade flourished, England began to prosper. Thereafter, within one hundred and fifty years, the monasteries were being abolished.

Translation of the Bible into the vernacular introduced newly personal knowledge of the word of the God and of the victory of Jesus, which spread widely but thinly. Comprehension was mostly not very profound. Protestantism (which literally means pro-testament-ism, giving precedence to truthful reading of Scripture over religious tradition and fashionable thinking) had a difficult birth. The Roman church regarded it as protest against its own learning and authority, despite the fact that many had endeavoured to change the Roman church from within. There was much resistance from vested interests. People found it hard to let go of traditions in which they believed themselves, often mistakenly, to have had security. And many envied those who had obviously found freedom and peace in Christ. Violence was generated by those with most to lose, notably Roman church authorities, and those with imperial power. Wyclif escaped with his life, although after he died he was declared a heretic and his body was exhumed and burned. Hus and Tyndale, and many others, were martyred, often by being burned alive. Rulers believed they had to control people's beliefs and minds by force so that their own version of Christian religion would engage God's grace for the maintenance of their imperial power and prosperity. (Indeed this same ideal, that all civilised people should be bound by one law under one imperial religious authority, remains very much alive today). Pictures by Durer, Grunewald and Altdorfer illustrate the extremes of those times. But by the time of Henry VIII the Bible in English was eventually placed in churches, and thousands were eager to learn the contents. Henry's minister Thomas Cromwell nevertheless paid with his life, in 1540, for having enabled the word of God to be known so directly by the people.

Naturally there was retaliation. Old ways die hard, people jump to premature conclusions and become legalistic, and Jesus said he had not come to bring peace on earth but a sword.[105] People of different prejudices fought each other, and dreadful mistakes were made on all sides In the face of duplicitous and violent attempts to be rid of Hussites, Cathars, Bogomils, Waldenses, Albigenses, and Lutherans, all wrongly accused of heresy, Protestantism soon defended itself by becoming institutionalized. Jean Calvin, a Roman Catholic lawyer, converted to Protestantism in 1533 and, extraordinarily quickly, became a powerful polemicist and preacher. He published "*The Institutes of the Christian Religion*" in 1536, and was invited to lead the city council in Geneva. Calvin was legalistic, effectively imposing on his adherents rules for sinless life, with belief in predestination and the futility of concern for souls not being saved (as if they could tell who they were) which they deemed to be idolatry of the flesh. But it quickly spread because of its plain use of the Bible, belief in justification by faith, clear definitions of right and wrong, advocacy of individual accountability to God and its rejection of Roman Catholic domination.

---

[105] Matthew 10:34.

Huguenots became a powerful force to be reckoned with in Europe. In 1534 Ignatius Loyola and Francis Xavier formed the Society of Jesus as a special force to defend the Roman Papacy. Then the Spanish Inquisition tortured and murdered thousands in a concerted and vicious attempt to annihilate Protestant and Jewish 'heretics.' Devastating wars were fought both on land and at sea. Although dominance in trade was always an additional motive, religious legalism was a driving force in European politics in the later Middle Ages.

There were thousands of oppressed and traumatized people, wounded in body and soul, and broken in spirit, whose main endeavour was mere survival. Many wandered throughout Europe. Yet there were many others who were able to take advantage of new discoveries, and who found opportunities to prosper. Ships improved; England built a navy; the world was circumnavigated. The Spanish took slaves from Africa to their mines and plantations in the newly discovered Americas, and imported silver and gold from there to expand their territories and pay their armies. But when Copernicus, a Polish Roman Catholic priest who lived from 1473 to 1543, discovered by mathematical calculation that the earth actually moved around the sun, he did not dare to publish his work during his lifetime for fear of life-threatening censure by church authorities.

Although the Bible addresses the whole wide range of human experience, interpretation of the Bible had been controlled by the institutional church in such a way that it was not so much applied to individual personal experience as taught as religious rules for living.

Furthermore, the Roman church violently resisted new thinking about new discoveries, although proper reading of Scripture would have prevented such abuses. It gave priority to imperialistic imposition of the dogma that had evolved within the institution, and had no qualms about inflicting suffering upon people who refused it. The gross hypocrisy of not allowing freedom of thought, and using violence and intrigue to maintain political power, instead of using dialogue and leadership, was apparent to those who knew Scripture for themselves. And whilst monasteries and convents were often philanthropic, offering help and hospitality to distressed people provided they did not openly challenge Catholic dogma, the church itself perpetrated terrible atrocities, was often corrupt, and generally failed to minister the healing described in the New Testament.

The new translations of the Bible, moreover, rendered Matthew 4:17 differently from the old Roman Catholic Vulgate Bible. The Vulgate said, "Do penance, for the kingdom of heaven is at hand." But the new translations said, "Repent, for the kingdom of heaven is at hand." (See the King James Version). So the new English Bibles spoke of inner cleansing of the soul by thankfully accepting the free grace of God through Jesus. But the old Catholic Latin Vulgate Bible obscured the gospel by requiring voluntary self-punishment and submission to penitential duties and good works, as required by a priest, from which the church profited financially through indulgencies.

So it is small wonder that scholarly people reacted to all this by seeking better ways of understanding. All sorts of doubts and arguments and debates developed amongst Christians, and others, about how to think in a way that was good and right. Luther fixed his *"Ninety-Five Theses"* to the door of the Schlosskirche in Wittenberg in 1517, declaring the Bible to be the true source of authority and salvation to be by faith alone, not by good works; and he renounced obedience to Rome. In strong opposition, Ignatius of Loyola's *"Rule 13,"* written about 1534, was entitled *"Rules for Thinking with the Church"* and upheld the authority of Rome. Jean Calvin had left the Roman church, and then published his *"Institutes"* in 1536. Petrus Ramus developed his *"methodus,"* a way of methodizing through dialectic applied to the search for truth in philosophical thinking, around 1550, and he subsequently left the Roman church, for which he eventually paid with his life. Between 1604 and 1609 the Protestant Jacobus Arminius publicly disputed with Calvinism, rebuking their judgmentalism and declaring the free grace of God to be available for all. And the philosopher René Descartes (1596-1650), who had been educated by the Jesuits and had become a soldier, as Ignatius had been, wrote *"Rules for the Direction of the Mind"* in 1628 and *"Discours de la Méthode"* in 1637, which he describes as a "discourse on the method of properly conducting one's reason and of seeking the truth in the sciences."

Descartes' method became enormously influential, and was soon applied not only to sciences but also to arts and to behaviour in general. Like others before him, Descartes had cast about for how to avoid doubt and be certain in his thinking; and he hit upon the realization that he could not perceive himself to be thinking without at the same time being certain of his own existence:

"Cogito ergo sum" ("I think therefore I am"). He recognized his own uncertainty, his own propensity to doubt, and concluded that doubt was an indication that he was an imperfect being. Since certainty was surely more perfect than doubt, he therefore reasoned that the gift of actually being certain of his own existence must have been given by a perfect being. Thence he calculated that God must exist and must be the author of his intuition. This belief remains surprisingly common to this day. But it avoids the Scripture which says that no one comes to the Father except through the Lord Jesus.[106]

So Descartes formulated rules for thinking whereby apparent facts ascertained through the senses are allowed to be enquired into and developed by the untrammelled guidance of logical reason, which he called "the pure light of the mind," to which he gave a divine origin. Under its influence analysis was made for the clear definition of facts. Then, with the help of memory and practical logical reasoning, thoughts were to be synthesized into understanding. And (like Plato) he believed the rational understanding and "truth" thus achieved could be held in the mind separately from the influence of the person's imperfect physical body.

Thus Descartes derived his "clear light of the mind" from his awareness of his own thinking existence, with all its theoretical influences. He endeavoured not to pay attention to the feelings, emotions, associations and meanings experienced in his living body, in his natural soul, because they caused him to doubt and appeared imperfect. He did not belong in a church for whom

---

[106] John 14:6.

natural reactions to this fallen world, including confusion, suffering and pain, had been taken by Jesus on the cross,[107] so that they could be confessed as sin and submitted to the Lord and healed by the transforming power of Holy Spirit, who comes when personal redemption is accepted through Jesus' shed blood. Descartes belonged, rather to a church that mercilessly imposed a system of mind control and contrived to dominate with its dogma. Therefore he did not seek direction from God through the Lord Jesus Christ.[108]

The method for certain thinking thus provided by Descartes has appealed powerfully to academics, and has been elaborated and commented upon very extensively ever since it was formulated. It powerfully influenced the "Enlightenment" of the seventeenth and eighteenth centuries, and the industrial development that followed. It has stimulated the systematic organization of business and politics, and has assisted massive developments in trade.

The social upheavals and misery eventually inflicted on thousands of people during the Industrial Revolution resulted in sporadic civil unrest, which was dealt with through political reform, the expansion of empire, and various systems of social administration and philanthropy, such as the building of workhouses, hospitals and asylums, and the eventual enfranchisement of all adults - all of which was influenced by Cartesian thinking. It is only recently, however, that science has developed technologies that

---

[107] Isaiah 53:4.
[108] Proverbs 3:5-6, Psalm 119:105, John 14:6.

have made the environment for human beings so very much easier than it used to be. So now we have reached a stage in which science and technology underpin the trade and continuous development and economic discipline that sustain the way of life described in the story at the beginning of this chapter.

It is worthwhile briefly to trace the way the spirit of Descartes' philosophy was extended by other philosophers and thinkers to become so influential in our own time. John Locke the philosopher (1632-1704), following Descartes, explained how he believed all knowledge to be derived through reasoning from experience.[109] He convinced people of the significance of personal perception. Those concepts in which we wish to express the elements of reality must be found in experience, including scientific discoveries. He did not deny that there was divine revelation but thought that revelation should be judged by reason and common sense. And he did not think anyone should claim to have a monopoly on truth. He was nominally Christian, and his attitude was rather more liberal than totally sceptical. He was very practical too; but although he was a physician he did not address suffering or healing of the soul. He could not explain how one person, or any spiritual being, could influence another person except by positing, like Plato did, that we follow instruction and instinctively know when things make sense. So it seems clear that he did not understand the personal nature of the spiritual dimension, and he did not specify how

---

[109]Locke (1690) *"Essay Concerning Human Understanding,"* Book II, Chapter 1, Section 2.

Jesus is the true light of the world. Politics was profoundly influenced, however, by his conclusion that if a pious nation was obedient to the church's teaching, following what was purported to be God's instruction, they would have good government.

Descartes and Locke were widely thought to have shown not only how to reason aright but also how to make value judgements. Their theories were soon applied to poetry and art. For a time it was believed that good sense and objective reasoning could engender talent, taste and virtue, and even provide the spirit for genius. The popularity of Calvinistic puritanism encouraged this attitude. The pictures of Nicolas Poussin (1594–1665) and Claude Lorrain (1600-1682) illustrate the idealistic purity of this gutless approach.

It could not last long in England, however, partly because Shakespeare (1564-1616) and Milton (1608-74) became popular as observers of ordinary everyday human nature. Their depictions of mankind were entertaining for many people, portraying with approval commonly accepted realistic facts of personal experience relating to everyday events that were always the subject of banter and comment. Thus as Galileo (1564–1642), and then Newton (1642–1727) used precise observations for remarkable advances in science so, in a similar way, sensitive and obviously accurate observations of everyday personal experience became relevant for British aesthetics. After the overthrow of religious dogmatism in the Civil War, people sought a more inclusive way to appreciate everything as fully as possible. They not only wanted beautiful clothes and manners and houses, but they also enjoyed the humour of street life. They studied the opinions of leaders of fashion who helped them understand how, with their increasing prosperity, they might enjoy order, truth and beauty in their everyday lives along with their liberated sensual pleasures. After the Civil War the majority would no longer accept an idealism that seemed abstract, austere or puritanical. They wanted an environment that spoke to them directly and that could pleasurably satisfy every human soul.[110]

The third Earl of Shaftesbury (1671–1713), who was one of the 'Cambridge Platonists,' influentially declared, "All beauty is truth." And he asserted that enjoyment of the beautiful is essentially a disinterested pleasure that is a creative function of the human spirit. Artistic genius had the capacity for inner agreement with the powers that formed and ordered the universe, so as to reveal the truth of nature through creativity. He said this was not subjective imagination requiring an emotional response, but rather a pure divine energy for the process of forming and creating, and in this spirit any emotion could be reasoned away into essential idealism.[111] Shaftesbury acknowledged the influence of Plotinus (204–270). And it is relevant that Plotinus had lived during terrible times towards the end of the Roman Empire, when the world of practical affairs had seemed

---

[110] Popular writers on the subject of Taste during this period were Voltaire, Diderot, Dubos, Bouhours, Boileau, Schiller, Moritz, Lametrie, Shaftesbury, Hutcheson, Ferguson, Hume, Addison, Burke, Hogarth, Kames and Baumgarten.

[111] Here I am particularly indebted to Ernst Cassirer (1932) *"The Philosophy of the Enlightenment."*

hopeless, and that he had chosen to isolate himself in a world of Platonic ideas and ideals, in which he believed happiness could be found through ignoring his own human body and despising the suffering felt and perceived through the physical senses. Plotinus' idea of "nous" was an openness of the human spirit to the light of the 'One' - the Divine Mind through which divine inspiration and empowerment come "beyond reason, mind and feeling."[112] The human soul possesses sufficient innate goodness, Plotinus believed, to respond creatively to ecstasy. Shaftesbury too celebrated a cosmic spirit which could be intuited sympathetically by mankind and used for a creative synthesis between mankind and the world in an aesthetic unity in diversity.

There are echoes here of Descartes "divine light of the mind." And Shaftesbury influenced the poet Schiller, who wrote *"Ode to Joy,"* which speaks of a uniting of all mankind, both good and evil, through the worship and the magic of a goddess. Beethoven set this poem to music in the last movement of his ninth symphony, and in this form it has now become the anthem of the European Community. But Shaftesbury failed to understand that according to the word of God, and to the experience of those who have truly accepted redemption by the Lord Jesus Christ, both mankind and this world is fallen.[113] We should therefore be very careful to discern accurately the spiritual origin of Plotinus' Neoplatonic divine light, for it has been a particularly profound influence, not only in the arts, the

---

[112] Plotinus, *"Enneads,"* V, 3, 14.
[113] Genesis 3, Isaiah 24, Revelation 21:1.

media and politics but also within all institutional churches both Catholic and Protestant.[114]

There had always been a cultural undercurrent amongst people who sought secret knowledge from hidden powers. Witchcraft has been common. Many country people knew about curses; and they also sought magic remedies from 'wise women' for ills and difficulties. Occult knowledge, communicated only to the initiated, was employed in alchemy. The secret society of Freemasonry, too, was widespread. In society at large there were consequently many opinions about the legitimacy of various means of enquiry, and about the true nature of events perceived through the senses that were mysterious and difficult to explain. Although the physician Paracelsus (1493–1541) used astrology and hermetic lore, he became for a time a professor of medicine at Basle. Even Sir Isaac Newton (1642-1727) one hundred and fifty years later was fascinated by alchemy. Salvator Rosa (1615-1673) achieved respectable popularity in some circles with his alarming but beautiful paintings of wild scenes, bandits, covens and the supernatural. In England the emotional, more traumatic and less formal side of life continued to be expressed in paintings by Hogarth (1697-1764) and later, rather more mysteriously, by Fuseli (1741-1825), Mortimer (1741-1785), and Blake (1757-1827). Sturm und Drang (storm and stress) became a fashionable artistic mode in Europe during the later eighteenth century, popularized by Goethe (1749-1832) and Schiller (1759-1805). About 1750 Horace Walpole, youngest son of Sir

---

[114] See the writings of Dean Inge, for instance.

Robert Walpole the first British Prime Minister, had enlarged his house Strawberry Hill in Gothic style, because Gothic was thought to be more primitive, mysterious and interesting than prevailing classical Greek formalism, and the fashion for architectural Gothic lasted to the late Victorian era.

Thus a reaction had developed not only against the dogma of institutional churches but also against obedience to the formality of deductive logic and mathematical reason and the associated stylized aesthetics. Powerful emotions of rejection, envy, want, pain, shock, horror, lust, confusion, and terror, were in truth the experience of multitudes of ordinary people as the result of violence, disease and privation, exacerbated by wars and social upheavals. And so it became fashionable amongst intellectual socialites to attempt to enjoy these same raw emotions in 'sublime' contrast with beauty, in an attempt to find ecstasy and creativity through vicarious epicurean abstraction. At least, the total 'sublime' effect added piquancy to sensual pleasure. Moreover the real facts of everyday human experience, which were often painful, were actually being accepted to some extent by literate sceptics in a less idealistic and rather more realistic manner.

The English Civil War had lasted from 1642 to 1648, and the subsequent restoration of a more liberal monarchy in 1660, followed by the peaceful revolution of 1688, placed a Protestant firmly on the throne and forbade the British monarch thenceforth from being Roman Catholic. The powers both of Roman Catholic religious dogmatism and also of Puritan Calvinist legalism had effectively been curbed. Social restraints had become more relaxed. Government gradually grew more tolerant. Trade and prosperity increased, and general education improved. Wars in Europe and at sea, however, were brutal. Through the East India Company, Buddhism and Hinduism and Islam became more of an intellectual influence. Society began to be industrial. Arable land was enclosed in order to feed the burgeoning populations of cities. Thousands of families and societies were disrupted. And more and more people knew the terrible reality of suffering through trauma of one sort or another.

Between the mid seventeenth century and the mid nineteenth century awareness of the more painful emotions of the body, and the reality of responses of the soul that sometimes seemed unreasonable, contributed both to the development of political liberalism and also to the flourishing of artistic romanticism. Philosophers developed theories to account for the various and sometimes extreme responses of the human mind and soul, and to incorporate them into some sort of hopeful and apparently practical vision, in order both to assist understanding and also to inform political administration. But they mostly took no account of the redemptive power of the Lord Jesus. Humanistic philosophy became an increasingly influential foundation for academic and political activity, and the institutional churches mostly forgot their first love and adapted their theology accordingly. Heartfelt compassion was reasoned away, in Neoplatonic fashion, to become pity. Charity likewise became philanthropy. Although John Wesley, and others with him, preached the real redemptive and transforming power of the true

Christian gospel, they were rejected by the majority of churches. And many of those whose lives had been profoundly affected by the Lord Jesus through those preachers quite soon became diverted into arguing about details of management, and into religious legalism, under the influence of the brilliant academic reasoning so often adduced in the changing times by men and women of practical affairs.[115]

The German philosopher Baumgarten (1714-1762) who was a son of a Christian pastor expanded the understanding of aesthetics beyond the limits defined by Shaftesbury to incorporate passions of the human soul, which he understood as vital impulses like the enjoyment of beauty. He said, too, that intuition could be more inclusive than mere concepts or reason, and that reality might be more adequately expressed through descriptive expression. In this he was perhaps the first phenomenologist. Language, for example, could dwell upon the nature of phenomena using intuition, imagination, judgement and inference in order to bring knowledge to life. Other artistic expression, such as painting, could do the same to a more limited extent. Scientific language, however, eliminates concrete content, he said, and its description of phenomena is, in fact, ambiguous because of its use of symbols. Baumgarten thus came close to speaking Biblical truth[116]

---

[115] See, for example, W.R.Ward (1972) *"Religion and Society in England 1790-1850."* See also Mark 4:17-19.

[116] See Deuteronomy 29:29; also 2 Corinthians 4:18, and 1 Corinthians 2:6-16. And the Christian philosopher Pascal said, *"The heart has its reasons, of which reason is ignorant."*

but, sadly, he persisted in idealizing beauty, and thus in expounding a doctrine of idealised human nature, which he failed to recognize to be fallen. Kant acknowledged his influence; and Kant in turn influenced Hegel, who profoundly influenced the rise of Germany, and who is still widely studied.

In 1762 Jean-Jacques Rousseau published *"Emile"*, also *"The Social Contract"*, through which he popularized his teaching that if we were honest we would follow feeling rather than reason, and base our beliefs on the emotions of the heart. Our natural feelings, he said, would lead us, without any need of revelation, to serve the common interest if we were to contract to forego our rights as individuals and take a place of equality with everyone else in our community and submit to the general will. These books helped stimulate the revolutionary spirit in France. And they were another influence upon Hegel.

So it became possible for the whole range of human experience and thought and creativity to be understood as being subsumed under a spiritual power that was *not* in fact that of the God of Abraham, Isaac, Israel and Messiah Jesus. And the subtle evolution of the work of this cosmic principality in human thought can be followed at least from the time of Plato in classical Greece to the days of Kant and Hegel, who both lived in Prussia and produced very detailed and extensive systems of philosophy that remain powerfully influential to this day They both spoke of spirit, and they gave widespread credibility to their notions of the transcendental and the absolute.

Immanuel Kant (1724-1804) became professor of philosophy at Königsberg. Whilst his *"Critique of Pure*

Reason" and his *"Critique of Practical Reason"* have led many people to assume he believed in God, or at least in some transcendental law above and beyond ordinary human experience, this was not the God of personal truth and justice, and of healing, peace and salvation, who communicates with people through Holy Spirit after they have accepted his only begotten son Jesus. Kant's god was deistic: although he was accepted as being there we could not really know him. Both pure reason and practical reason were developed from human experience for the purpose of controlling the world in which we people live. And although Kant implied that various aspects of divine law may be perceived through experience, and may affect the judgements we make, its basis for him was transcendental beyond human knowledge, and not arrived at either through acceptance of the Lord Jesus or from the word of God. For Kant the very notion of God was an impossible idea and metaphysical speculation was always doubtful.

Hegel (1770-1831), was professor of philosophy at Heidelberg and then at Berlin. He came after Kant and described a system of dialectic involving thesis, antithesis and synthesis by which we may progress to an integrative understanding. And he believed the ultimate synthesis to be absolute; that is, he believed the Absolute to be spiritual – one absolute, true, eternal, powerful essence available for human progress. A World-Spirit of Reason governs the world, unites with individuals and leads to freedom. Comparison with the Holy Bible reveals that this was not the Spirit of the God who sent his only begotten son to die on a cross for the sin of every person in the world, and who receives into the family of his kingdom those individuals who acknowledge their sin and gladly accept redemption through Jesus' shed blood, and who prove the resurrection power of their Lord Jesus Christ in their own lives through changes that become obvious. It becomes clear that the god invoked by Kant and by Hegel was certainly not the Father of the Lord Jesus.

During the nineteenth century, philosophers eventually stopped using their reasoning in attempts to prove the existence of God, as though that endeavour had finally become a waste of energy after Kant and Hegel. In 1789 de Sade roared rebellion to incite the mob outside the window of his cell in the Bastille, just before the Bastille fell, as the French Revolution gained momentum. In the face of such violence, philosophers' efforts became concentrated upon logical analysis.[117] It seems to have been accepted by them that the will of human beings could put into effect what appeared to be logically right, with the power to change society for the better. This was an assumption both of Plato and of Hegel. But it conflicts with Holy Scripture which clearly indicates that people can only have good lives after they make themselves right with God through recognizing and accepting, individually and in practice, what the Lord Jesus Christ has done for them.

So having arrived at an overarching logical acceptance that human nature could employ transcendent power from the Absolute in order to create a better life, the cosmic Platonic humanist spirit inveigled every

---

[117] This was pointed out by Bertrand Russell in *"History of Western Philosophy."*

academic discipline, including theology, into analytical and dialectical thinking from which new thoughts, new interpretations, new policies and new inventions might be synthesized – and one day, perhaps, even life itself.[118] Theologians, failing to discern the true origin and nature of the 'incomparably great power'[119] available to those who believe in the Lord Jesus, produced higher critical theology, which diluted the gospel with humanist ideas and in some respects turned it upside down. Utilitarianism produced the belief that actions are right if they promote happiness, and that policy should be directed towards the greatest happiness for the greatest number of people, which persists to the present day as a common belief. Medicine created institutions to house diagnosed illnesses and madnesses. Marxism produced the theory that material needs determine consciousness and will, and the resulting conflicts of social forces determine political and historical events (Karl Marx lived 1818-1883). Charles Darwin (1809-1882) produced evidence in support of the hypothesis that human beings could have evolved from simpler forms of life without the creative hand of God, and Herbert Spencer (1820-1903) coined the slogan "survival of the fittest" which in the popular mind was harnessed to trust in progress through human intelligence and ethical improvement. Such wishful thinking persists today.

Sigmund Freud lived from 1856 to1939, and his psychoanalysis confused the spirit of fallen human life with sexual libido. In consequence he discovered various

[118] Genesis 3:22.
[119] Ephesians 1:19.

unconscious psychological mechanisms which he intended both for scientific study and also for personal enlightenment. With William James (1842-1910) even religious belief was reduced to scientific psychological mechanisms.

As paternalism and aristocracy lost their dominance, political enfranchisement became necessary for all. As values were subjected to scientific inquiry, the politics of envy and equality gained momentum, and biblical doctrines seemed for many people to lose their relevance in favour of socialist activism. Religion tended to become either nominal or enthusiastic, and often of little depth.

The very nature of truth was questioned by Dewey (1859-1952) who substituted what could be revealed by inquiry for actual truth, and started the fashion for children learning experimentally from experiences provided by guided exploration. So now everyone has their own version of truth, and most people believe truth to consist of sceptically deduced facts, and any notion of truth being spiritual, or indeed a spiritual person, is almost universally dismissed.

Nietzsche (1844-1900) trumpeted extraordinary hubris when he repudiated Christianity and proclaimed the superiority of superman, and Wagner's music carried a similar message far and wide, thus preparing the world for two World Wars in which hundreds of thousands of people were used as readily expendable ciphers, and millions were systematically annihilated. And so the shaking of the world foretold in Haggai and Hebrews began.

Meanwhile impersonal logical analysis has been applied to every field of human endeavour, and has easily bestowed the illusion that if we trust academics and our own practical reason we shall be as safe as we can be and make progress. This ethos has encouraged hardness of heart. It has enabled people to avoid reflecting personally upon their own inner experiences, and laying them on the cross and waiting on God, thereby getting to know God better and developing in their hearts and minds sound personal understanding.

Objective systematic analysis has provided the rationale for exploring new avenues of thought, for doing things to enhance interest in secular improvements, and for gaining advantage for what is desired. The philosophy of Ayn Rand (1905-1982) advocated rational self-interest and has been addictively popular, exciting the adrenalin of millions. Objectivism is systematically applied to profit, using impersonal manpower on industrial assembly lines. It is applied to the human body which most people now treat as an object, as a machine to be managed with medical and psychological science and technology and understood no further (for the soul is no longer a valid concept). It is applied to medicine so that malfunctioning body parts can be fixed through human ingenuity. It is applied to information technology to give us artificial memory. It is applied to the impersonal management and manipulation of individuals. It is applied both to sexual activity and also to care, both of which are sold as commodities. It is applied to language so that now we may read things in various different ways because any way can be valid if it is amenable to objective reasoning.

It is applied to armaments to create weapons of mass destruction for the ultimate in attack and defence. It is applied to engineering to give us wonderful airplanes and cars. It is applied to farming to give us more food through genetic engineering. It is applied to politics to provide White Papers that inform policy.

The dream of one world order resulting from human endeavour is very much alive. The worldview created by secular humanistic objective analysis is the system unwittingly trusted by the man whose day was described at the beginning of this chapter.

There has been another philosophical movement, however, that has not received so much popular acclaim and has often been rejected. This movement has reflected a different, Judeo-Christian spirituality informed, however imperfectly, by the living God. True kindness, mature compassion, and love of one's neighbour, have been apparent in its discourses, despite being frequently disguised in intellectual and philosophical language. In the first half of the eighteenth century Søren Kierkegaard (1813-1855), a clergyman in the Danish church and a professional philosopher with a private income, not dependent upon any academic institution, wrote about body, soul and spirit, and about melancholy and sin, about anxiety and dread, and about love and hope. He described how suffering could lead, with God's help, to personal maturity, and he spoke of the holy rest that could be found through relationship with God. He distinguished between outward scientific observation and inward spiritual experience. He was particularly critical of Hegel, arguing that Hegel's philosophy was irreconcilably opposed to true Christian faith. Despite the soundness of his understanding of emotions, and of the autonomy and the inner spiritual nature of the individual person, his writing was not always easily understood because it was couched in philosophical language. He publicly criticized individuals in the church, furthermore, and his polemics brought him ridicule. He became isolated and died young; but his influence has slowly grown.

Franz Brentano (1838-1917) was a German philosopher who became a Catholic priest. He subsequently became involved in high level discussions challenging the declaration of papal infallibility and, in consequence of his challenge, eventually left the Roman Catholic Church. He taught that the characteristic that distinguishes mental phenomena from physical phenomena most significantly is intentionality. That is, mental phenomena are distinguished by behaviour originating within the individual and directed with meaning and motivation towards some object of desire or belief. Physical phenomena, in contrast, lack the ability to generate original intentionality. It seems this came to him when he was studying some medieval Christian scholastics along with Aristotle. However, it is noteworthy that amongst his pupils at the University of Vienna were Alexius Meinong and Christian von Ehrenfels, the founders of Gestalt psychology, and also Rudolph Steiner, and also Sigmund Freud, and each of these men went on to originate movements directed towards healing. It seems as though their compassion had been liberated by the revelation given to that Christian philosopher Brentano, who had made it possible for them to see that their interest in other people, and their desire to bring healing to them, could be reasonably accounted for philosophically. They became free enough in spirit to begin to try to work out how to put their desire for healing into practice with the sort of personal empathy for other people that takes seriously individual experience of emotions, perceptions and meanings.

From a Christian point of view they may each, to some extent, be seen now to have been misguided in their attempts to formulate their different systems of understanding; but it is noteworthy that they felt enabled to try to understand fundamental personal issues raised by human feelings and associated thoughts. They listened carefully, in detail, to the experience of ordinary people, and they recognized people's natural desires and reactions. Their concepts of healing included love of one's neighbour. The further logical analysis and understanding of intentionality undertaken by these men in effect included the sort of inquiry into human behaviour that Baumgarten had advocated, without following the broad, wide path of Kant and Hegel, and without invoking idealism, transcendentalism or the Absolute. I believe God had his hand on these men, and their followers, and has used them to speak to the human race about his love, and about his pain when his presence is disregarded. I believe God needed to use these people because the institutional churches by and large were unable to hear what God was saying in this regard, or to minister God's healing. And he has used them to give people hope so that they might see the way not only to come into his kingdom but also to be free. Too many people for too long have been lost, oppressed by the demand to be slavishly subservient, good and reasonable, and for too long they have been misunderstood, misled and distressed without substantial hope.

Edmund Husserl (1859-1938) also attended Brentano's lectures. Significantly, both Sigmund Freud and Edmund Husserl were Jews, so the desire and intention to love their neighbours as themselves had been inherited in their tradition.[120] Freud (1856-1939) claimed to be a secular Jew who had renounced belief in a personal God. In founding psychoanalysis he instituted a movement for logical analysis of the mind that he intended to be scientific, despite describing psychoanalysis as "essentially a cure through love."[121]

Husserl had voluntarily sought baptism as a protestant Christian after reading the New Testament. A profound sense of godly calling had come upon him then, although he never had anything much to do with any institutional church thereafter. At first he had been a mathematician but he became professor of philosophy at Gottingen and then at Freiburg. In 1933, although by then retired, he was relieved of all academic standing under Hitler's Third Reich. He strove to explain in philosophical terms the role of spiritual relationships in imparting knowledge, and to describe the useful but rather different place of abstract reasoning. He described empathy as the putative experiential awareness of

---

[120] Leviticus 19:18.

[121] Quoted from a letter from Sigmund Freud to his colleague Carl Jung, dated 6 December 1906. A copy can be found in *"The Freud/Jung Letters"* tr. Manheim and Hull, 1974.

another person. What the ideological theoretical philosophy of Hegel had termed synthesis could, he said, be understood in terms of intentionality. Husserl's 'phenomenology' was a descriptive accounting that was faithful to real everyday lived human experience. As with Kierkegaard, however, his language can be difficult for people who are not professional philosophers – for these men sought to be understood by other academics, if by no one else.

Husserl was a major influence upon Maurice Merleau-Ponty (1908-1961), a professor of philosophy at the Collège de France, whose description of a child's development during the first three years, in close relationship with the mother, remains profoundly moving and true to life. [122] Merleau-Ponty described and explained how we assimilate knowledge and meaning in our physical bodies (which he described as wholly animated) through being open to perceiving the presence of others and responding to them. He described science, furthermore, as naïve, dishonest abstraction (as had Baumgarten) making the point that our living bodies are in a permanent condition of experience, responding to our surroundings, and that it is artificial to separate mind and body and make a duality of them, as Descartes had done, and as most scientists have followed him in doing. Spirit, mind and body should not be separated.

---

[122] *"The Child's Relations with Others"* by Maurice Merleau-Ponty (1960) can be found in *"The Primacy of Perception,"* tr. James M. Edie, 1964.

This philosophical insight is highly significant for Christians because it corroborates James' contention that faith without works is dead.[123] Husserl, and Merleau-Ponty, and also Paul Ricoeur (who lived 1913-2005 and was a Protestant Christian philosopher, professor at the Sorbonne in Paris, and later at the University of Chicago in the Department of Divinity) have shown philosophically that what is experienced physiologically is made sense of in the living body through some degree of motor (or action) response, that is, through reaction involving some degree of natural motor activity according to perceived meaning, and which may or may not lead to overt behaviour. Physiological neurological connections are made with parts of the brain involved with memory, imagination and language; and these may lead to actual behavioural responses, which may or may not be conscious. Spiritual influences from past and present living relationships influence the nature of our responses. (For spiritually aware individuals this must include relationships with spiritual beings without physical bodies, as well as relationships with people, although of course these philosophers do not say this.)

Even though they couched it in academic philosophical language, these men spoke of spirit, and realized that individual people were spiritual beings with spiritual influence. They realized that relationships are spiritual, and that spiritual influences affect the living physiology of the individual body. They seem, however, to have had some difficulty explaining the nature of spirit to other academics.

---

[123] James 2:26.

Recent studies in the field of scientific medical neurology, however, vindicate their investigative philosophical descriptions. As mentioned in Chapter 1, mirror neurons are a distinct class of nerve cells that transform specific sensory information into a motor format and are found to play a role in action and intention and understanding and imitation and speech and emotion, in other words in the formation of meaning in the human mind, and meaningful communication with others.[124]

Of course there are many other people who have contributed their part in what God has been saying to us about his understanding of every aspect of our inner experience and about his longing to bring healing and peace to individual spirits, minds, souls and bodies. This is only a sketch; and filling in the details could be very much more extensive. The vast intelligence and loving generosity of Karl Jaspers (1883-1969), Martin Buber (1878-1965), Donald Winnicott (1896-1971) and Ronald Laing (1927-1989) should particularly be recorded, although there are many others. Such men have spoken the love of God deeply into the human condition in a period when the hierarchy of the church was unable to address the facts, having lost the biblical understanding of mankind, and therefore becoming deaf to what God was saying in this regard. As with all the others I have mentioned, however, in order to hear God through them it has often been necessary to transcend their

---

[124] Maddalena Fabbri-Destro and Giacomo Rizzolatti, *"Mirror Neurons and Mirror Systems in Monkeys and Humans"* in *"Physiology,"* 1 June 2008, Vol. 23, No.3, 171-9.

idiosyncrasies, for they have often felt the need to appeal to a specialist intellectual audience, and have often been less than perfect.

The relevance for Christians of this evolution of awareness, however, is highly significant. In these end times God is gathering people to himself who respond to his word in their hearts, in their physiology, in their souls. These are people who allow themselves to come alive to the presence of God, and alive in the kingdom of heaven, by accepting redemption from their fallen state through the blood of Jesus, and who love other fallen people despite the suffering it involves. What God is saying through his Holy Spirit to the spirits, souls and living bodies of human beings is now being heard more clearly and reaching fuller development. For the present it seems to be fourfold.

Firstly, it becomes clear that James, who said in his epistle that faith without works is dead, was not speaking about the sort of righteous works that are done to make a person seem to others to be dutifully good, but rather about the sort of actions that come genuinely from the heart of a person who is in a righteous relationship with the living God by being personally, knowingly, thankfully, and increasingly completely redeemed by Jesus' blood, and baptized in Holy Spirit. So James was not speaking of what has commonly come to be called charity and philanthropy but rather of an attitude of the changed heart, actively loving God with all the heart and soul and mind and strength all the time, in every aspect and respect, and loving our neighbours as ourselves in such a way as to bear one another's burdens so that each may carry his or her own load.[125]

Secondly, imparting knowledge of God and his word is best done through personal relationship that affects the heart and the deepest understanding, through engagement with the whole person in the sort of close, genuine and respectful relationship that the disciples had with Jesus, rather than through addressing the mind didactically from behind a lectern and filling a person with head knowledge and ideals that are never actually allowed to be processed in the heart and mind through the all the nitty-gritty of authentic living relationships. It is who is believed when all the facts have come to light that becomes truly significant, because the motor response is only remembered, and laid down as 'experience,' when who is believed is credible enough.

Thirdly, it can be seen that failure to live according to our maker's instructions, and allowing unclean spiritual influences to take root in our souls, may adversely affect our physiology and make us ill. Listening carefully, however, to what is on the heart of other people, in the presence of the Lord Jesus, will reveal in a truthful way what is hidden in the dark, so that it begins to make sense; and when it makes sense it is no longer mad, no longer beyond the pale, and therefore no longer so liable to make the individual ill. What is brought into the light in this way is by no means always nice, but it is not to be rejected. It is to be taken to the cross, and the atonement made by Jesus is to be accepted. When the person is made right with God in this way, and the acceptance of

---

[125] Galatians 6:2-5.

God, and the word of God, are then obediently and righteously acted upon, there will be deliverance, healing and peace. The past will begin to make sense in a new way, freed from its noxious hold on the person. So it can be seen that intimate but respectful fellowship with one another, as we come as disciples into the presence of the Lord Jesus,[126] will inevitably be healing if what is spoken, and thus comes to light, is put on the altar and offered up to him, and if we accept his redemption, and then use the authority he graciously gives us as children of God.[127]

Fourthly, since the word 'compassion' has come to imply an excuse for doing something to help with a sort of reflex condescending pity, lacking full fellow feeling, it now seems best for Christians to use Husserl's word 'empathy,' which implies the sort of fellow feeling that disturbs you, so that you have to deal with your own natural responses before God, and if necessary effect your own healing, in order to allow Holy Spirit to be the guide for your thoughts, emotions and behaviour with others without interference. Instinctively the other person will know the extent to which you know what is going on, whether or not you have empathy, disinterested compassion, love without strings, whether or not you are being in any way manipulative, whether or not you are leaving the other person free to make up their own mind, whether or not there may be personal advantages in pleasing you by behaving in the way you seem to want, and consequently whether or not real

---

[126] Matthew 18:20.
[127] 1 John 1:7; Mark 3:14-15; John 1:12-13.

healing and freedom are possible. If you are disinterested and godly, with mature understanding, you may actually seem threatening to some people, particularly to those who do not really know the Lord Jesus and have no knowledge of his love and his healing for emotions and thoughts. The opposition of some nominal Christians to this approach to other people's suffering can be nasty. They may become very defensive because they do not like to be challenged with uncomfortable disturbances. But the hard fact is that lack of faith is the main cause of reluctance to become involved with subjective issues relevant to sickness of spirit, soul and body. Unbelief and church tradition make it seem easiest to leave it all to the medical profession - most of whom practice only secular scientific medicine and are not Christian believers. So a new sort of church is necessary, a place where there personal, family, work and community issues can really be sorted out in fellowship together with God, where there is sound teaching from Scripture, and where he is worshipped in truth from the bottom of the heart.

*

The sort of experience of value to science has been experience of observation, measurement, experiment, objective classification, and systematic reasoning. What matters to science is objective experience. Incidents have often been experimentally contrived in order to extend inquiry and gain further knowledge. Facts are assessed in a guarded, sceptical way, and scientific relevance becomes apparent through abstract reasoning. Whilst doubt is maintained about the outcome of study, there will be some excitement about the possibilities of new discoveries. So very many new discoveries have come from systematic scientific analysis that seem to have made our lives so very much more certain and safe, by enabling us to fix our problems and control our environment, that abstract scientific thinking, and all the technology derived from it, has a valued place in our society. Medical science undoubtedly saves lives; and comforts many people, and provides the means for healing to take place in many cases that would otherwise seem hopeless. But scientific medicine does not address the spiritual dimension.

Christians have trusted science too much. They have presumed too often that the benefits of science and technology are the totality of God's blessings, without looking at the wider meaning and implication not only of scientific medical discoveries but also of the conditions being treated. They have presumed facts are truth without realizing that truth interprets facts. Subjective responses such as emotion, imagination, and the involvement of personal associations from the heart and mind, have not only been distrusted but often have been ignored and ruled out of court, as though God could never heal them sufficiently for his voice to be heard.

Of course, personal responses to events are often foolish or prejudiced, and sometimes they are extreme. Responses that give rise to offensive perception, doubtful meaning and disturbing behaviour are usually strictly controlled and restrained, often condemned and subjected to sanctions, or to some form of treatment, rather than considered before the Lord for healing. Sceptical philosophy, psychology and science have often seemed to be more reasonable, more acceptable, and easier to understand than the way of God, and to provide more trustworthy management and control to boot. Empathetic understanding and godly healing have, in consequence, mostly been replaced by abstract psychological, medical and theological theories. The result has been that Christian fellowships have often become nothing more than polite social clubs compulsively engaged in nice, kind activities. Thus churches have concurred with the apparent blessings of secular analysis and science by abandoning real faith, and no longer permitting their Lord to help them to see beyond the convenience of modern technologies and theories to the true state of each individual's soul, and then to give them faith for actual redemption and healing.

In a welfare state with scientific wizardry and political controls it can seem as though everything is well taken care of. The man whose day was described at the beginning of this chapter depends upon it, and he does not even notice how mechanical and secular his life is. He responds reflexly to immediate needs but never has the time for inner reflection. He shows little awareness of his deeper feelings, and minimal understanding of his motives. So who knows what hidden wounds need healing, or what his reactions would be if he were suddenly to be transferred into a totally different environment? No opportunity is afforded to make his life right with God.

What would he do if the very fabric of his life and of the society he lives in should be shaken again – as the word of God says it will be?[128] Would he recognize his spiritual poverty and his relative physical weakness, in the face of overwhelming calamity, and turn to the Lord for help? If he were inclined to do so, where would he find Christians willing and able to introduce the real Jesus?

I believe God is telling his people to offer hospitality and his healing to those who turn to him when they are shaken, and to help each other to work free from the deceptions of the world, and to seek to hear the pure word of God clearly, and to encourage each other to apply it in every detail of their lives.

""Because of the oppression of the weak and the groaning of the needy, I will now arise," says the Lord. "I will protect them from those who malign them.""[129] All conceit and sophistication and theory inevitably will be shaken; and the person and the words of God received directly in the heart of an individual, perceived through Holy Spirit and acted upon authentically, concretely, in truth, will bring freedom and healing.[130]

"When the foundations are being destroyed, what should the righteous be doing?" asks the psalmist.[131] They should have been holding out the word of life and shining like stars in the universe![132]

---

128 Hebrews 12:25-29.

129 Psalm 12:5.

130 Luke 4:17-21.

131 Psalm 11:3 (Lance Lambert's translation of the Hebrew).

132 Philippians 2:15-16.

Chapter 8 - Modern Relevance of Old Testament and Earliest Christian Doctrine of Mankind

God told Moses to tell the children of Israel, "Now therefore, if ye will obey my voice indeed, and keep my covenant, then ye shall be a peculiar treasure unto me above all people, for all the earth is mine. And ye shall be unto me a kingdom of priests, and an holy nation." (Exodus 19:5-6, KJV.)

At some level, every Hebrew knew this to be true – and they still do. They may try to deny it, but those with eyes to see know those irrevocable words are still being worked out today. The hand of God has remained upon His people. In fact, through their prophet Isaiah, He declared to them, "I have graven thee upon the palms of my hands." (Isaiah 49:16, KJV.) And in Genesis 17:13, speaking of circumcision, we have the words, "And my covenant shall be in your flesh for an everlasting covenant." Israel is at the heart of what God is doing. God's covenant with them is everlasting, as many other words of God make plain.

Yet Paul says, "Concerning the gospel they are enemies for your sake, but concerning the election, they are beloved for the sake of the fathers. For the gifts and calling of God are irrevocable." (Romans 11:28-29, NKJV.) In that passage Paul also writes that Jews have become enemies as the process of reconciliation to God has become available to the whole world through Jesus, and he expresses the hope that some Jewish people might be aroused to envy those who accept Jesus, and so be saved. Nevertheless Paul declares that we Gentiles, through being saved through faith in the Lord Jesus Christ, have been grafted in to the root of the patriarchs of Israel, and share in its nourishing sap. Therefore even though Jews may sometimes appear to be enemies and, by implication, Hebrew culture appear to be foreign, we should never jettison our connection with that root. In fact we should acknowledge that it actually supports us. Our freedom in Christ should never be used to root our salvation in revelation given through gods of Greece or any other pagan god. The only God worth obeying is the God of Israel, the Creator and King of the Universe.

Writing to the Colossians, Paul says, "Once you were alienated from God and were enemies in your minds because of your evil behaviour. But now He has reconciled you by Christ's physical body through death to present you holy in His sight, without blemish and free from accusation – if you continue in your faith, established and firm, not moved from the hope held out in the gospel." And later he says, "You have been given fullness in Christ, who is the Head over every power and authority. In Him you were also circumcised, in the putting off of the sinful nature, (that is, the flesh) not

169

with a circumcision done by the hands of men but with the circumcision done by Christ." (Colossians 1:21-23 and 2:10-11, NIV.)

God in His infinite love and mercy sent Jesus in order to rescue those who were lost, who were His enemies, and to make them a new creation, a kingdom of priests, and a holy nation. By His Spirit, God opens our ears and eyes and hearts so that we may understand Him; and He changes us and purifies us, if we will allow Him to do so, in order that we may become mature and equipped for our place in His eternal kingdom. Writing to the Thessalonians Paul prays, "The very God of peace sanctify you wholly, and I pray God your whole spirit and soul and body be preserved blameless unto the coming of our Lord Jesus Christ." (1 Thessalonians 5:23, KJV.)

So the sign that people belong to God was, and still is, that they are circumcised – either by the hands of men, as with the Jews (and some others) or by putting off the sinful nature by Christ, which is called by Jeremiah 'circumcision of the heart'. But Jeremiah in the Old Testament prophesies, '"Behold, the days come," saith the Lord, "that I will punish all them which are circumcised with the uncircumcised, Egypt, and Judah, and Edom, and Moab, and all that are in the utmost corners, that dwell in the wilderness, for all these nations are uncircumcised, and all the house of Israel are uncircumcised in the heart."' (Jeremiah 9:25-26, KJV.)

Therefore the only circumcision that will count before God at the last will be circumcision of the heart. Interestingly, Ezekiel calls the circumcised heart a "heart of flesh" as opposed to a "heart of stone". (Ezekiel 36:26.)

Those whose hearts have welcomed the Lord Jesus Christ have warmed human hearts of flesh, hearts of understanding through the Spirit of God living in them, hearts that are feeling, not hardened; aware, not deaf and blind; not shut off in denial but open to truth; and sure that whatever suffering may ensue will be carried by Him who "took up our sicknesses and carried our pains" (Isaiah 53:4). We thank God that we may cast our cares on the Lord, for He will sustain us (Psalm 55:22, 1Peter 5:7). Circumcised hearts come alive. We have a heart in every vicissitude, a heart to give thanks and praise. Even though we may suffer, we may hear God speak to us and be guided and encouraged.

Thus by 'suffer' we mean 'allow'. We allow God to be in charge, knowing he knows what we are going through, and knowing we belong with him. As when Jesus said "suffer little children, and forbid them not to come unto me, for of such is the kingdom of heaven" (Matthew 19:13, KJV), so He allows us into His encouraging, healing, life-giving presence when our hearts are open. He takes our pain and He carries it. But that does not mean we are to deny our feelings, for that would be to harden our hearts and deny our sufferings, which would make us unreal. The burden is His, if we belong to Him; but He wants us in our bodies learning from him and getting equipped in this world until He takes us out of it. As with Job, our sufferings change us, and bring us to new places of worship, repentance, understanding and wisdom (see Job 42:1-6). With hearts of flesh, we may know His presence throughout whatever we suffer.

Those who receive the Lord Jesus Christ as their Saviour, and receive the seal of Holy Spirit, and continue to know His authority for purifying their flesh, that is their whole spirit, soul and body, will live for ever - "born again, not of perishable seed, but of imperishable, through the living and enduring word of God." (1 Peter 1:23, NIV.) The implication is that the circumcision and warming of the heart done by the Lord Jesus will lead to a process of making right with God every part of the spirit, soul and body. "If the Spirit of Him who raised Jesus from the dead is living in you, He who raised Christ from the dead will also give life to your mortal bodies through His Spirit, who lives in you." (Romans 8:11, NIV.) Even the living, mortal body is affected.

Those who really belong to God are those who tremble at His word and are poor, humble, and contrite; (Isaiah 66:2b). They are those who allow themselves to suffer. Both trembling and suffering are physical. They involve physical discomfort that might cause some alarm to other people and might even be called 'illness' in modern parlance. I remember once being asked by one of the leaders of our church if a woman who was doing a lot of trembling at the word of God was perhaps mentally ill. I knew her a little, and knew she loved and sought the Lord, but she could be seen to be trembling like an original Quaker sometimes, God bless her! And to have questioned her sanity, or to have called her ill, would have been to put a massive stumbling block in the way of what God was doing in her life. "Thus saith the Lord, 'The heaven is my throne, and the earth is my footstool: where is the house that ye build unto me? And where is the place of my rest? For all those things hath mine hand made, and all those things have been,' saith the Lord, 'but to this man will I look, even to him that is poor and of a contrite spirit, and trembleth at my word.'" (Isaiah 66:1-2, KJV.)

There are churches that are respectable and properly behaved according to the expectations of polite secular society, sometimes delightfully behaved according to the expectations of the religious. They are fond of glorifying God and singing joyful songs and appearing happy and loving. And just occasionally you may find a church group who are hospitable to how people really are, and who seek the face of the Lord in their everyday suffering, which may sometimes be severe, and who sincerely know the heartfelt joy of the Lord, and His presence and rest and healing despite everything, and who actually reveal His true glory. These are the churches wherein the Lord can make His home and purify individual spirits, souls and bodies without misunderstandings and prejudices, and the hardness of people's hearts, getting in the way too much.

There is an apostate church and a true kingdom church these days – in fact the two exist together - and in the parable of the weeds, in Matthew 13, Jesus tells us to let both grow together till the harvest, in case the one be destroyed with the other. But the Lord should not be hindered from purifying our spirits, souls and bodies by the respectable prejudices, stereotypes, diagnoses, or other manifestations of Greek, scientific, secular or pagan thinking of others. "Hear the word of the Lord, you who tremble at His word. 'Your brothers who hate you, and exclude you because of my name, have said, "Let the Lord be glorified that we may see your joy!" Yet they will be put to shame. Hear that uproar from the city, hear that noise from the temple! It is the sound of the Lord repaying His enemies all they deserve.'" (Isaiah 66:5-6, NIV.)

Our concern is for those grafted in to the spiritual root of the patriarchs of Israel, those who have circumcised hearts that have come alive through accepting the Lord Jesus Christ, and Him crucified to save them, and His blood shed to redeem them and make atonement for them. Like Jesus, they will be made perfect through suffering (see Hebrews 2:10-18). Once they give their lives to the Lord, all that befalls them will be for building godly character and hope through endurance and perseverance (see Romans 5:1-5). It is those who overcome the world by the grace of God in the power of the Holy Spirit who will inherit the kingdom of God (Revelation 21:7).

In order to understand all this, we need Hebrew ways of thinking rather than the classical Greek ways of thinking prevalent in our present-day secular scientific culture. This is because ways of thinking that are essentially Greek deal with the anxiety of not truly knowing by classifying experiential data. So a false, abstract and theoretical system is developed, that can easily seduce us into believing we understand and really know, when in reality we have only classified, measured, quantified and collated data available to our senses in order to develop and use technology for the manipulation and control of our situation.

For example, a man develops a tight pain in his chest that seems to constrict his breathing. He consults a physician, who diagnoses 'angina', and orders various tests, and prescribes drugs that relieve the pain and distress. Medical technology is life-saving, brilliantly clever, enormously effective, and worth paying a lot of money for. But Jesus' healing is free. 'Angina' is a Latin word for the strangling pain about the throat that we used to call 'quinsy', and it comes from a Greek word 'ankhone' meaning 'severe constriction, or strangling'. Etymologists tell us these words are connected in their origin with 'anger' and 'anguish' and 'anxiety'. The Latin word 'angere' means 'to cause pain'. Doctors have given a Latin name to the condition, which makes you believe they understand what is going on in your body. This is an old trick that boosts the prestige of the medical profession no end. But in truth a deeper understanding can be found by calling on Holy Spirit, listening to your own body, allowing yourself to be aware of your condition as a whole, and consulting the dictionary. The doctor's sort of understanding enables him to provide technology to alleviate the condition. Certainly that has a most significant place for our lives. But it does not address the root of the trouble and heal it.

How many attacks of angina have been caused by sudden anger, worry or stress? When I was a junior doctor working in a hospital's Intensive Care Unit I remember a man whose chest pains were so intense and uncontrollable that we eventually sent him for one of the first heart transplants. What I particularly remember about him was that the affairs of his heart were most exceptionally tormented because, effectively, he had two wives and two families, with whom there had been a great deal of deception and misunderstanding.

I am not insinuating that everyone who has a heart attack has a difficult love life, for the heart is the centre for far more than one's sexual relationships; but I do suggest that if you have a heart attack it is worthwhile to endeavour to be reconciled to God regarding all the affairs of your heart, in the broadest possible sense. And I am also suggesting that a similar attitude should be taken with regard to all other illnesses, and that enormous benefits can ensue as we take to God the issues from which our physical illness may stem. If we learn to connect our thoughts and memories and feelings and emotions with their physical effects in our living bodies, and then open our hearts to God, accepting that His only begotten Son, the Lord Jesus, allowed His blood to be shed to redeem us, and died to save us, and rose from the dead, and now sits at God's right hand to intercede for us, then we shall walk in repentance and faith into healing, and our lives will change. There is a depth of repentance connected with all this that God wants His people to come into, so that He can equip them with understanding for His end-time purposes.

The sort of understanding that the physician is equipped with, that produces the medical technology that he uses to treat your complaint, comes from a system of analytical thinking rooted in ancient Greece. Scientific technological medicine is essentially abstract, an example of secular scientific humanism, and dissociated from the whole lived reality of the person. It does not take account of the whole human being. It does not make connection with related thoughts and memories, feelings and emotions, or with the related truth of social relationships in such a way as to take into account true meaning. It treats the illness in a way that is disconnected from everything else that is going on for the person. It treats the diseased part of the body in a way that denies its function as a part in the whole life of the individual. It is mechanistic, and treats the body as a machine. It is the latest manifestation of the classical Greek notion of the body as physical matter and the prison of the soul, of the duality of matter and spirit, whereby the body is evil, and never endued with any living divine goodness.

This is the thinking that gave rise to early controversies about the divinity of the Lord Jesus, notably Docetism, which was the belief that Jesus was pure spirit and his physical appearance was an optical illusion, which the disciple John warned us about in his first Epistle, when he said, "Test the spirits to see whether they are from God…every spirit that acknowledges that Jesus Christ is come in the flesh is of God, but every spirit that does not acknowledge that Jesus Christ is come in the flesh is not of God; this is the spirit of antichrist." (1 John 4:1-3, KJV & NIV.)

That sort of dualism was developed out of speculation about the nature and uses of matter, and an uncertainty about divine revelation. Such speculation led to denial of the powerful pagan influences in play beneath the surface of rational humanism. After all, the Greek gods seemed to behave like vindictive human beings, only with supernatural powers. So they could easily be ignored, and their influence could easily be dismissed as mere superstition, when speculation and experiment led to effective theories affording such enormous apparent benefits to mankind.

At the time of the Enlightenment, the realm of theory began to be remarkably extended through the use of the microscope and telescope to pry into the then unknown. By now all sorts of data can be examined in all sorts of inquisitive ways, and made use of to enhance our experience, and our speculations and our technological abilities in so many dimensions, that some philosophers say with good reason that we human beings now have the power to transform the world and make everything all right. Some of us, however, can see that this would involve living in total simulation and virtual reality, disconnected from God. Although he would still be in ultimate charge, our dismissal of him would not only remove us from his blessing and protection but plunge us into divine wrath.

How, you may ask, can the hand of antichrist possibly be found in such wonderful blessings as the provision of drugs for angina, and heart transplants, and Elastoplast, and Cognitive Behavioural Therapy and other clever, scientific, mechanistic treatments?

By seducing us into simply accepting such powerfully effective tools whilst at the same time ignoring the Creator and King of the Universe who sent his only begotten Son, The Lord Jesus Christ of Nazareth, to redeem and save us, and give us eternal life; and by saying that all our medical and technological benefits are God's provision so we need look no further, least of all into our own hearts, lest we find it disturbing!

The psalmist wrote, "Lord, my heart is not haughty, nor mine eyes lofty, neither do I exercise myself in great matters, or in things too high for me. Surely I have behaved and quieted myself as a child that is weaned of his mother. My soul is even as a weaned child. Let Israel hope in the Lord from henceforth and for ever." (Psalm 131, KJV.). Quiet comes to the soul from God's healing.

In contrast with the classical Greek tradition, the Biblical Hebrew tradition, with the hand of God upon its development, is that God formed a man in His own image out of matter, "out of the dust of the ground, and breathed into his nostrils the breath of life," *neshama*, "and he became a living being", *nephesh* (Genesis 2:7, NIV.). And then God made woman from the man to be a helpmeet. So both man and woman were made in God's image and received life from the breath of God. They were called Adam and Eve, and their spirit was obedient to God, their Father, until they were seduced into disobedience by the devil in the form of a serpent. They were seduced into eating from the tree of the knowledge of good and evil, although God had said they would die if they did so. Their disobedient rebellion, and their forbidden knowledge, generated an abiding human pride in endeavouring to make the world a better place in their own strength and by their own devices. But their spirit – *ruach* - died; and from then on mankind has been a fallen race.

By accepting the animal sacrifices made by Adam's second son Abel, and rejecting the fruits of the soil offered in worship by his older brother Cain, God made it plain to mankind that they would be accountable to Himself for their lives, and it was a life for a life. All people were vegetarian in those days, so the requirement to sacrifice animals must have been a revelation from God. Animals had the breath of life in them as well as people. The sacrifice of an animal would

179

be sufficient acknowledgement, for the time being, that they owed their lives to God. People became naturally aware of their vulnerability and covered themselves with animal skins to protect themselves.

After a time, some people began to call on God. But most people were so wicked that eventually God destroyed everyone in the great flood, all except one righteous man, Noah, and his family, together with all the animals Noah collected in his ark. After the flood, God told the people they could eat animals; but He forbade them to eat blood, because the life was in the blood (Genesis 9:4, Leviticus 17:11). Life-blood percolated through every part of every sentient body. And God demanded an accounting for the life of every human being.

Animal sacrifices continued to be offered to God in worship, in order ritually to atone for sin and guilt, and to celebrate in fellowship before God, until the destruction of the temple by the Babylonians about two thousand five hundred years ago. God had accepted animal sacrifices in making covenants with his people, and animal sacrifices were re-instituted with the building of the second temple. But they ceased when the temple was destroyed in 70 AD, although they have continued to this day in one or two odd places. But by that time the Lord Jesus Christ of Nazareth had already, Himself, become the ultimate sacrifice, and had obtained eternal redemption by His own blood for those people who truly believe in Him (Hebrews 9).

Thus, for both Hebrews, and Christians, God is always to be approached with blood, and is to be feared. He is also available to be called upon. Christians have the advantage in knowing that their redeemer made himself the sacrifice for them with his own blood. Those who have an assurance of this can approach God without guilt and with confidence (Romans 8:1-4).

God is central; his person is the absolute frame of reference. He is the King and Creator of the Universe. It is in Him that all things hold together (Colossians 1:17).

Each one of us will stand before God to give our account and be judged (see Revelation 19-20). "Nothing in all creation is hidden from God's sight. Everything is uncovered and laid bare before the eyes of him to whom we must give account." (Hebrews 4:13.) There will be an accounting in truth for every detail of the life of each one of us. Jesus tells us that we shall be accountable even for every careless word spoken (Matthew 12:36). Therefore we would do well to keep short accounts with God now, by walking in repentance and faith all the time, fully aware of every aspect of our lives, every aspect of our spirits, our souls and our bodies, not only so that our sin might be forgiven and forgotten and healed by God in this life (see Hebrews 10:17) before we stand before him in the next, but also that we may be healed and equipped to assume the place he has for us in his eternal kingdom (Matthew 19:27-30).

Chapter 9 - Protectionism

God once told the prophet Ezekiel to confront Jerusalem with her detestable practices, which God described as even more depraved than those of Sodom. We all know that the sins of Sodom were sexual.[133] But it is not immediately obvious why Ezekiel should have written, "Now this was the sin of your sister Sodom: She and her daughters were arrogant, overfed and unconcerned; they did not help the poor and needy. They were haughty and did detestable things before me."[134]

Most of us would probably admit that the connection between aggressive sexual sin and being too arrogant to be concerned about the poor is not immediately apparent. Spiritually minded people may point out that the people of Jerusalem had blatantly worshipped other gods, and had therefore committed spiritual prostitution, and that such behaviour had brought about the natural consequences. For those who do not understand how worship affects behaviour, however, further explanation is necessary in order to be more

---

[133] Genesis 19.
[134] Ezekiel 16:49-50.

credible. So something of the psychology and psychodynamics must be described, and some account must be given of what might go on in people's souls and minds and bodies for haughty disregard for the poor to be connected with predatory sexuality.

The sort of events that occur to make a person bitter, and to harden the heart against other people's feelings and needs, even to the extent of appearing haughty, are the sort of painful events most people do not want to have to think about. Bad things happen and cause pain. They happen to almost everyone, and occasionally they can be very bad indeed, producing powerful emotions, and reactive behaviour that is distressing. People commonly prefer to try to bury the memory, and the associated thoughts and feelings, and to dissociate themselves from it all for fear of being overwhelmed by the effects of dreadful events, and of being dismissed, misunderstood or rejected when strong emotions are expressed about what has occurred - and also for fear of not being allowed to reflect on it all, so as eventually to find healing and come to terms with it in their own space and time. They then try to maintain their self-control through will power, habit, and avoidance of anything that reminds them. People will automatically keep distressing feelings out of their minds, except perhaps for a token remembrance. They will say, for example, "My father left my mother when I was ten, and two years later, after he went to live abroad, he was killed in a road accident. He was a lovely man. I could not go to his funeral. But I went to see his grave a few years ago." But they will not dwell on the real pain, or the deeper memories or the details, for fear of being unable to cope with all the feelings that might come up, and with all they still mean and imply. A lot of those feelings, such as guilt and fury and rejection and hatred and terror, often seem utterly intolerable, especially if they are about someone you actually love, or someone other people respect. Their manifestation would not be considered polite in respectable society because others may not know how to cope with such a display of emotion. Shows of such madness, and the consequent social rejection, may discourage other sufferers, too.

From a person's earliest days wounds are formed in the soul in this sort of way, however, and they can become areas of lasting sensitivity. Wounds due to loss, or rejection, or due to violent invasion of personal boundaries, or domination or manipulation by others, or due to effectual cursing or unjust accusation, can remain buried unhealed throughout life. They fester because they are never exposed. People will often refuse to go there, and they will forbid memories of such hurtful experiences to surface, and they will avoid circumstances that could remind them. Because they arrange their lives in such a way as to protect the sensitive unhealed areas of their souls from being troubled, their relationships with other people may become difficult, however, and all sorts of unclean spirits may be attracted to them as they try to enjoy themselves by behaving in ways that are socially acceptable, and at the same time endeavour to appease their desire for diversionary entertainment. In this sort of way, wounds from old traumatic events, and from the things done for protection in case anything like that ever happens again, and also wounds from some of the things done for pleasure in order to relieve boredom and depression, will lie among the skeletons hidden in the cupboard of the soul until there is healing. Many people believe there never could, nor even ever should, be effective healing for such feelings, memories and fearful sins. It is dreadfully common for people to mock the very idea. Living with the grudges they bear, with their prejudices, and with the wounds they have suffered, becomes a way of life. But the spirit and the soul and the mind and the physical body will inevitably be adversely affected in consequence.

Whilst such guarded behaviour lasts, people will spend their energy on making themselves feel good if they can, rather than on actually involving themselves with anyone who may make them feel uncomfortable. "Why not look on the bright side?" they will say. And many other people will tell them, "Why not enjoy yourself? We don't like you going around looking morbid! Why not make positive lifestyle choices that give you some pleasure?" So it becomes habitual to seek what feels good. It becomes part of your culture for negative feelings to be considered sick, and for it to be bad to have baleful emotions. "Never mind what all that horrible stuff means; don't think about it!" "Jesus took it all on the cross. Don't think about it!" "If you are still suffering, why not go to the doctor and get a prescription for your nerves?" And for those not constrained by Christian ethics: "Why not use some of these recreational drugs?" "Why not enjoy things that excite you?" "Why not watch this film?" "Listen to this music!" "Why not have the sort of sex you fantasize about?" Having given in to such temptations, the excitement, the thrills and the relief rapidly become addictive, and the desire for more becomes almost impossible to resist. If you know others who get excited doing the same sort of thing, it becomes socially acceptable for you. But if what you have been doing is seriously challenged, and you begin to feel guilty, it becomes very tempting to defend your position and make it impregnable. In an arrogant show of strength you say, "We don't want people around here who make us feel bad. People who are different from us make us angry. Why not have fun at the expense of those losers who cause trouble for us? They're not really alive, not fully human. They're just pigs!" "Why not treat them as scum, and just use them and take their property? We'll do what we want with them!" "What matters is survival of the fittest." "We are entirely justified in what we do!"

That is how unredeemed human nature works, and how sexual sins become associated with neglecting the poor. When people cannot face their own pains and sins they lose the ability to feel for others. Even if personal defences shatter, even if well-meaning people put help and constraints in place to modify and control people's behaviour through social welfare programmes, through enfranchisement for democratic government, through legal sanctions, through education, through media, and through religious dogma, human nature has the capacity to remain in this mode. Beneath the surface our natural fallen human nature remains capable of the most terrible evil unless our nature is changed.

Unredeemed human nature is found both in people who are secular and also in people who are religious. Secular people will mostly conform to social mores, and use reason, psychological theories, will power and medical science, in order to try to be good - with plenty of pleasure seeking. And a lot of old wounds will remain unhealed amongst them. Unredeemed religious people will allow themselves to be dominated by religious rules of conduct, codified to keep their fallen nature in control, which can be successful so long as they maintain a close relationship with their church, although many of their activities will be more or less secular.

In contrast, those people who genuinely know themselves to be redeemed by the blood of Jesus, and who maintain a living personal relationship with Holy Spirit, will discover themselves to have power to work free of thoughts and behaviours that offend him.[135] They will come to discover that self-control is a fruit of the Spirit that causes the hooks of temptation to fall away from them, which relieves them of stress.[136] They have freedom, revelation from the kingdom of heaven, and peace. The Spirit of Jesus is radically different from the spirit prevailing in the world.

So who are the poor and needy? Are they not those who are less able to cope with their own failings, those who are most vulnerable to the domination and oppression of people who have managed to be more successful through competitive aggression and worldly guile? Naturally those who take pride in their successes will have little reason to question their own behaviour or to recognize their own poverty. It is amongst the genuinely poor and needy that it seems more probable

---

[135] John 1:12.
[136] Galatians 5:22.

that there may be some who seek spiritual help and healing, and who would accept it from Jesus if they could find it. Some may even be inclined to enquire into the scriptural meaning of their condition. And Jesus says that if they would turn to him he would bless them and the kingdom of heaven would be available to them.[137]

Of course, it will make it easier for everyone to live together peaceably in society if the poor are assisted philanthropically with material goods. This would be a political act influenced perhaps by Christian ethics. But it may or may not encourage their ability to survive and find salvation. For many centuries churches and charitable people have offered practical help to people who have seemed to be in need of it. And ever since the French Revolution the poor and oppressed have become more successful in their demand for better secular consideration. They have been appeased with enfranchisement and welfare services. Love of one's neighbour, even for Christians, has come to mean catering materially for the indigent. Knowledge about poverty has accumulated through objective analysis of systematically collated facts, and political and sociological solutions have been put in place. Indeed after the time of William Wilberforce (1759-1833) the word 'charity,' which originally implied real Christian grace, kindness with disinterested understanding, and the sort of compassionate love that enabled people to be personally accountable in truth, and free to carry their own load,[138] rapidly became secularized and associated

---

[137] Matthew 5:3.
[138] Galatians 6:2-5.

with pity, so as to mean voluntary gifts of money and goods to help people lacking means of practical support.

Ezekiel described the iniquity of Sodom as compounded not only by refusal to help the poor in a practical way but also by pride and lack of concern. With generosity of heart the concern he spoke of can lead to kindness and to awareness of how the other person is feeling and thinking. But degradation of the meaning of the word 'charity' has corresponded with degeneration of disinterested Christian compassion. After all, which is easier: to give money, or to show empathetic concern by attending with discernment and opening the heart to feeling the other's pain without being overwhelmed? To be sure, to do something practical to help has often seemed to be the most urgent necessity; but the ability to empathize with disinterested love in Jesus has often been absent. Ethics have taken the place of personal love of one's neighbour.

In fact the ability to understand and encourage the process of spiritual healing of the soul has largely been lost for two thousand years, confounded by classical Greek philosophy and systematic rationalism. The search for understanding of the human condition during the nineteenth and twentieth centuries has been confined by academic reductionism. The Spirit has been quenched. Plain understanding of the Bible has often been stopped and its truth distorted. The haughtiness and pride embodied in the rules of conduct of traditional institutional religion have caused legalistic demands for compliance to be substituted for godly compassion, understanding and hospitality. Churches have protected themselves from getting their hands dirty, and from the personal emotional discomforts of loving one's neighbour as oneself, by claiming their good governance depends on avoiding worldly contamination. Repentance is needed.

When there is no provision in a society or culture for the personal healing of feelings, memories and thoughts, there are many aspects of themselves that people prefer not to face. When there is no provision for the healing of bitterness and fear, people will guard themselves by adopting attitudes that protect them from the possibility of opening old wounds. And if that security seems threatened, they can become very nasty in self-defence. Even if they claim to be religious, their system of belief will commonly have been adjusted to their prejudices so they may have great difficulty in allowing any suggestion that other points of view may be valid, or that they themselves bear hidden wounds that are unconsciously influencing them. It says in Proverbs that, "Pride goes before destruction, a haughty spirit before a fall."[139] And when, sooner or later, the fall comes and personal defences are shattered, some of them may become psychiatric casualties. If they give a thought to calling on the Lord who heals, they will probably not be healed all at once. They will probably need extensive help and encouragement if they are ever to see things God's way, because change of mind is a slow and complex business. And they will need to be careful about whom to believe. Secular help will be available - but it is becoming impossible for secular psychiatric and counselling facilities to be staffed by genuine Christians.

---

[139] Proverbs 16:18.

Human nature is only radically changed in itself after receiving the Holy Spirit and allowing him to begin, and to continue, a transforming work in every aspect of one's being. Holy Spirit will come when access is given to the Father's throne room through simply and personally accepting Jesus' redeeming sacrifice for our fallen human nature and sin. His new nature is then bestowed upon us by Holy Spirit, and we find ourselves empowered to persevere and endure and overcome and become more like our maker. This is how it is under the New Covenant these days, after the coming of Messiah.[140] But there is so much mistaken theology, and so much worldliness, in churches that it is often necessary not to rely on teachers but rather to allow Holy Spirit to be the one to open the Scriptures privately to the understanding. The whole Bible can be read in one year by reading one chapter of the Old Testament, one psalm, and one chapter of the New Testament night and morning, beginning at the beginning and working through to the end.

The first five books of the Bible tell how the Spirit of God was at work in the Jewish nation from its beginning. Repentance and forgiveness for healing became known in ancient Israel.[141] The law given by God through Moses catered for the poor.[142] Love of one's neighbour was known,[143] and the love of God, too. The Jews were chosen people, and they still are, whether

---

[140] 2 Corinthians 5:17.
[141] As witness, Psalm 51 and 2 Chronicles 7:14.
[142] As witness: Leviticus 19:18 & Deuteronomy 15.
[143] Leviticus 19:18.

they like it or not.[144] Those who lived in a way that was right with God were blessed with peace and sufficiency;[145] but those who lost their righteousness were disgraced and punished.

Jesus addressed these issues in the parable of the sower[146] where he showed how unclean spiritual influences, and the inability to use adversity to gain wisdom and understanding through waiting on God, and the worries of this life, and the deceptions of wealth and of apparent ease, may prevent the seed spoken into the ground of a person's life by the Spirit of God from bearing fruit.

As for natural emotional reactions to events of every description, from slaughter at one extreme to love-making at the other, the Bible describes them all. The Bible describes, too, how we may find constant healing for our natural emotional reactions through living in relationship with God. Emotion was, and still is, very much part of everyday life for all Hebrews. The notion that every thought should exclude emotion in order to be reasonable is a terrible deception, the result of centuries of persuasive classical Greek, Neoplatonic and scientific influences in philosophy being adopted in academic theology, church tradition, medicine, politics and the arts, and spreading into general acceptance.

Life without reactive emotion is dead. Emotions arise naturally within the living physical body in response to what is going on. Meaning develops naturally through

---

[144] Jeremiah 31:35-37.
[145] Deuteronomy 7:12-15.
[146] Matthew 13, Mark 4, Luke 8.

the involvement of memory stored in the body, influenced by past and current relationships, including worship. Fantasies develop naturally in the imagination. All the thoughts are modified to some degree by awareness of what seems socially appropriate. Thoughts mature in the mind, and affect behaviour, and are modified by experience. And the Bible tells us to take every thought captive and make it obedient to Christ,[147] which we can only do if Christ who redeemed us with his blood is present, which he will be if we maintain a living relationship with him through Holy Spirit. The Bible also speaks of forgiveness and casting all our cares on Jesus, saying that Jesus took our pains and sicknesses on the cross, and when he comes to live in us we shall already have been healed by what he suffered,[148] so we should act on that fact in the power of his Spirit who has defeated death and destruction. But of course this depends on faith, on believing in him. The faith that concerns us here depends on acceptance of the victory over Satan, death, this world and the flesh, won by our Lord Jesus on the cross. This faith is strengthened as we allow ourselves to be open about what we think and feel, and bring it all to light, not denying the true facts, so that all that is in our hearts and minds is healed in the power of Holy Spirit.

The writer of Hebrews tells us not to fall away through unbelief, but rather to persevere with hope and courage, pointing out that the Lord Jesus himself learned

---

[147] 2 Corinthians 10:5.
[148] Isaiah 53.

obedience through what he suffered.[149] Thus we too are to learn obedience through what we suffer, even our poverty, wounds, confusion and sickness. This certainly does not mean we should not have emotions. But it does acknowledge that allowing our emotions to come to light may involve suffering. And suffering is only possible if there is hope. Without hope in our hearts there is only pain; but when there is hope there is always the possibility of light at the end of the tunnel, even if we cannot see it, and of healing. So when we have hope it becomes a matter of working through what has to be gone through with endurance and perseverance.[150] The God of Israel, the God of love, sent Jesus his only begotten son to enable us, when we accept what he has done for us, to enter God's presence where there is no curse, or guilt, or death, or pain. From his presence flow rivers of living water which bring new life to a person, with love, peace, discernment and spiritual authority. So Paul prays for the Roman Christians, "May the God of hope fill you with all joy and peace as you trust in him, so that you may overflow with hope by the power of the Holy Spirit."[151]

So we can see that those who have been baptized in Holy Spirit, and who continue to live in Holy Spirit, will be willing and able to meet whatever comes their way and deal with it righteously, with compassion and

---

[149] Hebrews 5:8.
[150] Romans 5:1-5.
[151] Romans 15:13.

understanding. The world is full of trouble, and they will overcome through the Spirit living in them.[152]

But if they endeavour to overcome solely through their own cleverness or strength, or through the world's systematic science, or through adherence to religious rules, they will be liable to lose their way.[153] It behoves us always to ask ourselves whether or not our understanding represents premature closure, and whether it has been salted with wisdom through kingdom revelation. The classifications and categorizations of systematic science are convenient and useful; but they are abstractions, and they contain an element of protectionism that we can hide behind, and thereby refuse to open our minds to what God would have us do with what we have found. The legalistic mindset of church denominations can serve the same sort of purpose, generating tradition that quenches the Spirit instead of allowing people to respond in the Lord to their experience so that they may grow in personal maturity.

Christians are enabled to face the world when they have Holy Spirit living in them. They then have the power to be salt and light in dark, unhealthy places.[154] And God's grace is sufficient for them.[155] So there is no need for Christians, when properly equipped, arrogantly to protect themselves behind secular custom or religious tradition. They will be guided by Holy Spirit.

---

[152] John 16:33.
[153] Zechariah 4:6.
[154] Matthew 5:13.
[155] 2 Corinthians 12:9.

Prescriptive legalism is a particularly dangerous protection against the world because it poses a peculiar challenge to people who are sore from worldly battles, people who are not feeling at all good in themselves. It invites a contest with ideals that claim to be of God, to which they are effectively told they should match up, although it is always plain to see the inherent hypocrisy that results. Christianity has so very often failed to be credible because it is not seen to do what it claims to do, namely to heal and to change lives. So often all people see is a bunch of religious actors whose lives fail to be authentically fruitful with love, joy, peace, patience, kindness goodness, faithfulness gentleness and self-control, according to the word of God in the Bible. Not only does this make people feel sore, and potentially ashamed, but naturally it excites mockery, anger, accusations of hypocrisy, and worse. Prescriptive Christianity is readily recognized by spiritually aware pagans as inauthentic. They can recognize nominal Christians who are acting the part and who have a form of religion without the power. They know how ill equipped such people are, and how vulnerable when hardship faces them, and they know that they can easily be picked off. Because the factual head knowledge of nominal Christians has not been anchored in their souls through personal experience of living out in faith what Holy Spirit says, and by learning from their experience so as to work out their salvation with fear and trembling in personal relationship with Jesus,[156] tragedy may ensue. Hiding behind the defensive lines of prescriptive

---

[156] Philippians 2:12; Acts 19:13-16.

religious rules and traditions naturally leads to entrenched positions and prejudices, for fear of the challenges. People who do not develop a personal root of understanding easily fall away.[157] This is why baptism in Holy Spirit is so important.

Jesus was always brilliant at meeting and answering all the questions, needs and taunts to which he was constantly exposed. His replies came from his Spirit, out of relationship with his Father, rather from deductive reckoning and head knowledge. He was always on the alert and ready to move. He would often answer a question with a question, invoking personal relationship and inviting ongoing conversation. He went where the Father told him to go and did not look for trouble, although if others made trouble he answered them plainly and without excess emotion. Sometimes he escaped suddenly and walked through the crowd without being attacked. It is worthwhile to take especial note that he told us that if people in one place do not accept our peace we should let our peace return to us and shake the dust of the place off our feet when we leave,[158] He also said that all people will hate us because of him, and that when we are persecuted in one place we should flee to another, and that we shall not have finished going through all the cities of Israel before his return in glory.[159] In the garden of Gethsemane he demanded that the soldiers let his disciples go.[160] He

---

[157] Mark 4:17.
[158] Matthew 10:13-14.
[159] Matthew 10:23.
[160] John 18:8-9.

prophesied, however, that some of us would be betrayed and persecuted and handed over for trial and punishment, and be put to death because of him. And he said we should be on our guard and stand firm to the end.[161]

It is apparent from his teaching that a flexibility is demanded of us, an ability to be shrewd, to parley with salted speech, and to know where to go and where not to go, and when to leave. There seems to be no point in being defensive, in becoming entrenched in a position, or in standing on one's dignity; it is better to escape. Living like this a person would suffer perpetual insecurity unless they have a real living personal relationship with God the Father through the Holy Spirit.

Experience of troubles in the world, however, is always bound to produce emotion and stress to some extent. Emotion is a physical and spiritual response to the perceived meaning of events, and concomitant stress occurs in the physical body. Meeting unexpected, difficult, threatening or unfamiliar situations demands careful sensitivity and perspicacity with ready resources of discernment and wisdom. Being on one's guard demands heightened alertness. Since Jesus seems to expect his disciples to be ready and able to decide rapidly what to say and what to do, whether or not to get out of a situation, or whether to endure the inevitable, according to the Father's will, we need to stay in good shape and remain as unencumbered as possible, because living in this world demands energy and fitness.

---

[161] Mark 13:9.

To separate what is physical from what is spiritual, or to separate emotion from physiology, or to imagine that religious faith is all in the mind, or is an ideal in the heart that has no effect on the living body, is artificial, because the one aspect goes with the other in the whole living individual. To expect that Christians should live in the world and not be affected by it but remain nice and polite all the time is unrealistic. Our bodies will be adversely affected, nevertheless, if we get it wrong, and so will our thinking. Getting it right means always involving God; therefore baptism in Holy Spirit is essential. Perhaps it is necessary these days, however, to reduce such concepts to elements that are more readily understandable so that the whole meaning may be comprehended more thoroughly.

Emotion and stress are not comfortable, as the modern world understands comfort. If the Spirit of God is present, and the situations that produce them are handed over to God, however, the peace of God comes, and events will be handled righteously provided we have allowed ourselves to be trained in righteousness as disciples, and are not simply dispassionate observers. At the end of a day full of emotion and stress from challenging situations, it will usually be necessary to rest physically, and to catch up and reflect on the day and pray, like Jesus did when he went off alone to quiet places.[162] The residue of emotion will need to be processed by making adequate sense of all that has occurred, discerning truth and deception, forgiving and seeking forgiveness, and seeking understanding and

---

[162] Mark 1:45, Luke 5:16.

wisdom in the healing presence of the Father. This is what Jesus meant by shaking the dust off one's feet. At the end of a week of it, the Christian who has been active as salt and light in the world will be glad of a Sabbath, a whole day of rest and healing with loved ones in the presence of God. It is not, therefore, that stress is bad; what counts is how we deal with it.

It is impossible to meet others without some degree of stress, or to be real without emotion. Any pretence of being unaffected in a human way by events of personal relevance, any pretence of being able to handle everything in a rational way without emotion, or of being compassionate without feeling what the other person is going through, will naturally be felt by other people to be to some extent insulting. People who are religious in a legalistic way may give the impression of being right with God by adhering to a set of religious rules of conduct, or by following ritual, but they will often fail to affect the heart of the other person so as to encourage true understanding, healing and peace, because they will be cold and inauthentic. At some level it will be discerned that their spirit is out of kilter with their mind, so they will not altogether be believable.

People protect themselves in this sort of detached way, however, when they have never been able to find true healing and peace for themselves, for the feelings and thoughts inside them, because it has never been possible in their lives to bring them all into the light. Some of the truth of their experience remains hidden. In order for it to come into the light, and be revealed, they must permit themselves to be allowed and received, warts and all, by others. In healthy families this occurs naturally in childhood. But many families wittingly or unwittingly impose rules that the children are never really allowed to make sufficient sense of. This can bring defeat and exasperation into the hearts of the children, and hidden rage, which may remain until mother and father can be constructively criticized and forgiven. In many people the resultant bitterness and confusion remain throughout life. Naturally, then, it will cause them to be legalistic in turn towards their own children.

Legalism is its own worst enemy because it judges the thoughts and emotions and experiences and perceptions of others, and thus suppresses them instead of allowing them and engaging with them. Thus they remain suppressed in dark places to cause trouble later, and the person lives with areas of life that cannot grow to maturity. Those dark places, furthermore, may lead to a deterioration of health, due to chronic unknown stresses, with associated fantasies and temptations, so that resilience is compromised. The pervasive effect of unhealed stresses can be found in every illness.[163]

Experience of the world in a person whose personal perception has been refined by Holy Spirit will fill that person with wisdom from God, so that the person is not only authentic but also sanctified, made holy. Sanctification is a lifelong continuing process in which the Holy Spirit is allowed to move into every area of the

---

[163] Henry W. Wright's book "*A More Excellent Way – Be In Health - Spiritual Roots of Disease and Pathways to Wholeness*" is recommended. My own book "*Healing for the Wounded Life*" also deals with this subject in some depth.

soul so as to change every aspect of the whole person, to equip the person for God's eternal kingdom. As the individual perseveres in keeping short accounts with God, responses to worldly reality become habitually righteous. The person matures as a new creation. This is how we become equipped for our eternal place, reserved for us with the Father. The presence of God will be reflected in that person's life, and the potential for healing and truth will live in that person and affect others.

This is not to judge a person a sinner if he or she is ill. We are all sinners, and we all get ill from time to time, and some of us have inherited deformities that are stubbornly resistant to healing in this world. When we love our neighbours as ourselves we love fellow sinners and encourage each other in persevering with the Lord. The fact is, however, that when we accept Jesus with grateful hearts we are made not guilty, justified through Jesus' blood, and allowed into the presence of Almighty God "just as if we had never sinned." We are enabled by Holy Spirit to get to know him, and gain entry into his kingdom where there is no sickness or pain, and we receive power to become children of God and to overcome. God's kingdom healing remains available to us in this world, and we endeavour to appropriate it by getting rid of what gets in the way of living in the presence of Jesus. Our behaviour, therefore, depends ultimately upon our spirit rather than on the reasoning of our mind.

Whilst some of us have allowed ourselves to be discipled and disciplined with healing love by Holy Spirit, others have listened to the teaching and have tried to apply it through mental effort but have not been moved in their hearts by the author of the teaching.[164]

Perhaps we can now understand how treating the mind as separate from the body can result in disconnection from God's person, resulting in a religion that is only intellectual, in which God's ways are known in the mind from Bible teaching, and even lived out obediently according to received instruction, but not actually embodied so as to be applied in the world, for real, applied to personal thoughts and feelings and behaviour, to one's very flesh, so that God's ways may become natural and the person becomes a new creation maturing in authentic holiness. It is possible for the meaning of God's words to be taught, and considered in the mind in academic depth and complexity, without being applied in the living body through really getting to know the author. This protects the person against the person of the author through natural dissociative physiology that prevents one yielding one's soul to another. Yet the Holy Spirit is the person who can make all the difference between life and death. And knowing God's person through receiving his Spirit is possible only through genuine, simple, meaningful, personal acceptance of God's merciful provision for our fallen nature and sin by sending his only begotten son Jesus to pay the price with his own blood to redeem us, and by continuing to work out our salvation in thankful, loving relationship with him in every aspect of our lives. And this way there is healing, too!

---

[164] Matthew 25:1-13.

The Bible warns us in many places against being deceived. And the whole of the letter to the Galatians is a warning against legalism, which Paul equates with witchcraft. A lot of religious people act the part they think others expect of a good Christian. They say all the right things and behave in a religious manner, and may even be overtly evangelical, without having allowed the Holy Spirit to change their thinking processes. Their thoughts and feelings and patterns of behaviour have not been laid on the cross. So the presence of the living God is not revealed through their physical bodies. And because they neglect themselves in this way they fail in compassionate involvement with the poor.

This is an easy mistake to make in modern Western culture, in which the way we think about ailments and suffering is scientific, and secular authorities provide for our welfare, academic institutions regulate health care that provides for every sort of distress, and the way you actually happen to believe is seen as a lifestyle choice within the confines of totalitarian government control. Yet there are still a few people who can see how being looked after through government that appears to be democratic, and endeavours to give people what they want, may actually be a preparation for oligarchs to take over. It is time for kingdom people to open their eyes, to stop allowing themselves to be deceived, to wake up and offer people the Holy Spirit's healing to free their minds. There is no need for this to interfere unduly with the usefulness of academic study and scientific innovation. Our scientific and technological achievements are necessary these days; but it is foolish to depend on them alone.

It is time for Christians to come together in fellowship together with the Lord Jesus to encourage one another in true healing and holiness, instead of being religious. The genuineness and effectiveness of such meetings will depend on accurate discernment of the signs of the times and on everyone being honest before the Lord about their own, often painful, experience. Prophecy and healing are vital.

There has always, of course, been some degree of righteousness, albeit all too often didactic and legalistic, or even wayward, in churches throughout the world during the two millennia since Jesus came; and to a remarkable extent Christian churches have been a measure of salt and light in the nations where they have existed. But under opposition and persecution they have so very often effectively compromised with the enemy, and have even sometimes reacted with violence, and have failed to rally together sufficiently to wait upon the Lord effectively and receive his direction and healing. The vast majority of people who have called themselves Christian throughout the past twenty centuries have clung to dogma and religious tradition without prophetic insight, having a form of Christian religion but so often denying the power. There have been dreadful arguments over hermeneutics, and appallingly violent persecutions as one faction has sought to dominate another or to maintain freedom to worship in the way they believed to be right. Political rulers have commonly perceived worship as a threat to their ability to control their populations - although they have almost never acknowledged this openly – and they have manipulated control of religion through dealings with popes and bishops and leaders of other religions. Of course this has been a tacit acknowledgement of the reality of spiritual power, although they never acknowledge that either. It seems fair to state that politicians instinctively protect themselves against the power of religious faith by endeavouring to control it. And churches, most notably the Roman Catholic Church, have protected themselves by creating religious institutions and making compromises with politicians. When the controls have become so severe that even conventicles have been forbidden, the alliance between church and state has been particularly dangerous for genuine believers. The few authentic Christians have often had to make drastic arrangements, or move on elsewhere, when opposition has made life too difficult. Some have been trapped in impossible situations and atrociously persecuted. Thousands have been burned alive or otherwise murdered, even by other so-called Christians. Persecution continues to this day.[165]

General freedom of worship will only be found where biblical Christianity (not just the tradition of one institutional branch) is given a dignified place in the state, and where the state allies itself with the benign justice of the Holy Bible.[166] It is significant that this has

---

[165] See, for example, *"Cox's Book of Martyrs"* by Baroness Cox.

[166] Psalm 45:6 says, *"Your throne, O God, will last for ever and ever; a sceptre of justice will be the sceptre of your kingdom."* And not without reason Proverbs 16:7 says, *"When a man's ways are pleasing to the Lord he makes even his enemies live at peace with him."*

been possible to a large extent where the Anglican Church has been established, and the monarch has been non-interfering titular head. Malign forces, however, have made dangerous headway recently in undermining this arrangement, with the help of academic Bible criticism and replacement theology. Anglicans have suddenly lost godly toleration of many of the issues raised in this book because they have failed to heed prophetic warnings. Their discernment has been faulty and ecumenism has tempted them powerfully to unite under the banner of Rome. Christians moving under the direction of the Holy Spirit often cannot join them because the hierarchy lacks the capacity to hear what is said with true discernment, and tries to control what they do. Future trouble in both church and nation is therefore to be expected. Protection for Spirit led Christians is being removed; and as freedom of worship is undermined it will be necessary for Christians to be on their guard and to receive and act on supernatural wisdom. They may need to meet in secret. They may need to move house. They should look, therefore, most carefully to their own healing and equipping.

As the end of the age draws near, the Holy Spirit enables us to cut through all the philosophical reasoning and false religion, and transcend our modern dependence on media culture and secular welfare. The Lord Jesus, the only begotten son of God, overcame our fall from grace, overcame the sin of the whole world, and opened the way for us to the kingdom of God, and to the almighty person of God, when he died on the cross and rose from death the third day after. Holy Spirit is available to those who accept the Lord Jesus Christ personally, for real, as their redeemer, confessing their sin and accepting atonement through his shed blood. Holy Spirit opens eyes and ears and hearts to perceive differently from the world, differently from churches that compromise with the world, and differently from churches that compromise with each other's legalism through ecumenism. Holy Spirit breaks through deceptions and defences, and provides comfort when what is revealed is painful, and gives gentle power for healing. Holy Spirit bestows the discernment necessary for disinterested love and compassion, and bestows the authority to speak God's words both into nice situations and into nasty ones. And Holy Spirit enables his people to respond with love to God the Father with their whole heart and mind and soul and strength in this world, and to love their neighbours as themselves.

It is vital for those coming into the kingdom of God that the healing work of the Holy Spirit should not be prevented by academic reasoning, nor by seductive ways of thinking, or of worshipping, perpetrated by people who are in fact protecting themselves by all sorts of compromises against challenges and difficulties in this fallen world, rather than patiently waiting on God. Spirituality not based in genuine individual acceptance of what Jesus Christ did on the cross, worked out in practice, even sometimes in the very worst circumstances, is bogus. We need to be able to discern when plausible people do not really know what they are talking about, or truly mean what they say. And it is best for genuine Christians to meet in fellowship, for that way it is easier for disciples to encourage each other and work free within themselves. Sadly, however, there is so much deception in the world that many Christians may need to find their way in relative isolation. If we persevere and overcome we shall nevertheless see Jesus. The word of God from Isaiah 57:14 and 19 is, "Build up, build up, prepare the road! Remove the obstacles out of the way of my people." "And I will heal them."

Chapter 10 - Application

In his book *"Beyond Good and Evil,"* published in 1886, the philosopher Friedrich Nietzsche said, "...a thought comes when "it" wishes, and not when "I" wish; so that it is a perversion of the facts of the case to say that the subject "I" is the condition of the predicate "think."" It therefore follows that Nietzsche was aware of thoughts coming into his mind that were not consciously calculated or regulated.

And there was also, of course, an implied reference to Descartes' famous "cogito ergo sum" with the implication that, although thinking makes us aware of ourselves, we are actually lived by forces that may be unknown.

A little later, because this experience seemed common to mankind and relevant to their study of mental distress, the psychoanalysts separated this "it," or "id," from the "I," that is, from the "ego" (which perhaps may be described as the face of the person who engages with the world). They then set about trying to prove that the powerful, and perhaps mysterious, personal influences that are hidden under the surface of the ego are only human.

Yet despite psychoanalytic theory about libido and life instinct, the agency of what comes to mind from this "it," or "id," still remains controversial for many people.

When an individual is moved to accept into awareness thoughts that seem to come from somewhere other than conscious reason – thoughts which may be embarrassing, passionate or tender – or when an individual happens to make connections with emotions of which he or she had been previously unaware, then there is activity in the abdominal cavity that can actually be heard as unusual borborygmi. These sounds are particularly noticeable if a stethoscope is applied to the abdomen. The bowels move as though there were a release of resistance. And vocal utterance, too, may be surprising. Instinctively, other people may feel compassion, or may at least be merciful enough to have greater understanding of that individual - which might even cause similar movements of the bowels in them. These are the bowels of mercies and compassion referred to in the old King James Bible (see 1 John 3:17, etc.). Polite society, however, usually finds such events rather disagreeable. And secular society dismisses their significance. Because such matters are misunderstood they may be offensive, so they are commonly hidden from view.

Yet Isaiah calls to God, "…where is… the sounding of thy bowels and of thy mercies toward me? Are they restrained?" (Isaiah 63:15, KJV). And Jeremiah cries out: "My bowels, my bowels! I am pained at my very heart; my heart maketh a noise in me; I cannot hold my peace..." (Jeremiah 4:19, KJV).

Neither ancient Hebrews nor ancient Greeks knew of the function of the anatomical diaphragm, the muscle dividing thorax from abdomen inside the body cavity. They did not separate thorax from abdomen. They envisaged the visceral area as a whole, called the bowels. So the heart was reckoned to be in the bowels. This is illustrated in Psalm 22:14: "...my heart is like wax; it is melted in the midst of my bowels." And children were born from the bowels ("...thou art he that took me out of my mother's bowels..." (Psalm 71:6)).

For the Hebrew, thoughts came from the heart, and had motives in response to events. Jeremiah (Chapter 17 verse 9) said, "The heart is deceitful above all things and beyond cure. Who can understand it?" And Jesus said, "out of the heart proceed evil thoughts, murders, adulteries, fornications, thefts, false witness, blasphemies." (Matthew 15:19, KJV). So it seems reasonable that the thoughts and emotions and gut reactions of human nature, which lie under the surface, should be excluded from polite society.

According to the word of God, human nature is fallen and sinful (Genesis Chapter 3). But in Luke 2:35, Simeon, regarding Jesus, prophesies that, "...the thoughts of many hearts will be revealed." Jesus "knew what was in man" (John 2:25) but he preached repentance and healing for sin. In the kingdom of God, which we may enter through accepting the sacrifice of Jesus, there is forgiveness and healing for all the thoughts of the heart. Jesus' blood was shed as he went to the cross to pay the price to redeem every sinner who would accept his sacrifice and receive his Holy Spirit with a thankful heart. He said, "... if the Son sets you free, you will be free indeed." (John 8:36.)

God had declared to Isaiah: "Go, and tell this people, Hear ye indeed but understand not; and see ye indeed, but perceive not. Make the heart of this people fat, and make their ears heavy, and shut their eyes; lest they see with their eyes, and hear with their ears, and understand with their heart, and convert, and be healed." (Isaiah 6:9-10, KJV). Thus understanding, too, is located in the heart, as well as thoughts; but the heart can become unresponsive, fat, calloused or hardened.

It seems that the Hebrews, both in the time of Isaiah and in the time of Jesus, accepted that thoughts coming from the bowels, in response to experience of events, could be cut off from awareness and not understood. People would thus become blind to what God was doing, and to the full truth and significance of what was going on.

Now that anatomical science has made us aware of its nature and function, however, we can see how the diaphragm plays a part in this. Restriction of the movement of the diaphragm makes breathing shallower, restrains the movements of the alimentary canal, alters the circulation of blood, and may effectively keep certain thoughts and emotions suppressed. If you need to stop yourself saying something, your breathing changes slightly. Such restriction of free movement of the diaphragm can be seen to affect our wellbeing and physical health if the bowels are troubled or pained for too long.

The nerve that supplies the diaphragm muscle is called 'phrenic.' That name comes from ancient Greek 'phren', meaning heart or mind. The name not only indicates the regulation the mind imposes via the diaphragm, but it also indicates the validity of locating thought in the bowels.

A little later than Isaiah, classical Greek philosophers, notably Anaxagoras, Plato and Aristotle, began to develop a significantly different way of understanding the nature and functioning of the human mind. According to their line of reasoning, the mind makes judgements about what is perceived through the senses. With this information it is possible to reason, to classify, to deliberate, to form concepts, to endeavour to establish causes, and thus to develop a systematic understanding, in the hope of finding goodness, usefulness and truth. The agent doing this sort of controlled thinking is conscious human reasoning, with the brain as dominating agent of control.

Problems became apparent, however, because there is always doubt. The consequent difficulties have kept academics busy for centuries. How is it possible, in a socially acceptable way, to order and control the emotions associated with perceptions? And since we only actually see in part at any given moment, how accurately do we conceive of wholes, of essences, or even of ideals? Is what we perceive actual reality? Should perfect understanding be best achieved through geometry and mathematics? And what is truth? And what is goodness?

Since the Renaissance of Greek learning which began about the twelfth century, and particularly since the so-called Enlightenment, it has seemed advantageous for the senses to be used to observe, classify and measure every possible detail of our world. Classical Greek ways of thinking have prevailed amongst philosophers, academics and politicians. Schools and universities systematically train the mind in secular humanistic reasoning with concepts reckoned useful for human advantage and survival. We expect science and technology developed from such ways of thinking to provide relief of hardship, efficient administration and all the seemingly necessary continuous improvements. Most of the psychological and psychiatric management of people who are judged to be excessively disturbed depend upon this systematic way of understanding, too. Bowels of compassion are in short supply.

What counts as thought for the secular world is conscious calculation. The mind has come to be conceived of as rather separate from the everyday experience of the living body. Thoughts of the heart that are not clever, not expressive of pride in human ingenuity, tend to be ignored or denied. After all, abstract theoretical thinking is less discomfiting than dwelling upon gut feeling.

The gods and the humanism of classical Greece have never been able to connect people with truth sufficient to heal human nature. Therefore those who recognize their fallen condition, and who want to change and be saved out of it and find healing for spirit, soul and body, and healing for their relationships, must find their way beyond the deceptions inherent in the cultural heritage of classical Greece, beyond many concepts taught in academic disciplines, and often beyond secular medical diagnosis. To be successful, their quest must involve reconnecting with personal experience and gut feelings, opening their hearts, and "Casting down imaginations, and every high thing that exalteth itself against the knowledge of God, and bringing into captivity every thought to the obedience of Christ." (2 Corinthians 10:5, KJV).

If Biblical Hebrew ways of conceiving 'mind' were more readily understood to be separate from the classical Greek ways prevalent in our culture, many people seeking effective Christian encouragement and healing would be saved from secular psychology and psychiatry and much physical illness.

A living human being in Hebrew is *nephesh*. Spirit is *ruach*. *Nephesh* and *ruach* are sometimes used interchangeably so that an actual person can be called *ruach*, indicating the central involvement of a person's spirit in relationship. Suffice it to state that God has *ruach*; people have *ruach*; animals have *ruach*. *Ruach* is also used of breath, or of wind. It is also used of emotions, like "anguish of *ruach*" (Ezekiel 27:31), or of demons, like the "evil spirit" that came upon King Saul, recorded in 1 Samuel 18:10. The spirit conveys living personality, an individual formed in unique detail in a living moving feeling body, who is present amongst other people and things and events. The body is physical in the case of human beings and animals, but spirits and demons have spiritual bodies – their form is not of the dust of the earth. And God holds everything together.

The spirit of an individual may be weakened by distress of one sort or another, whether troubled feelings (as in Psalm 6) or hunger or thirst (as in Psalm 107:4-9); and this is the basis of Paul's doctrine that we cannot put our confidence in the flesh (Romans 7:18): "I know that nothing good lives in me, that is, in my sinful nature. For I have the desire to do what is good, but I cannot carry it out." We have inherited a dead, or fallen, spirit from Adam and Eve that causes our flesh to behave in a weak and unredeemed way. We retaliate, we bear grudges, we repay what was done to us, one way or another, according to the mores of this world, and we become subject to diseases and sicknesses prevalent in our sick societies. And only when we are met by the Lord Jesus, and repent, and accept Him for our Lord and Saviour, and are born again, and receive an infilling of Holy Spirit, do we find the power to overcome our fallen nature. Then our *ruach* is reborn of God, and through Holy Spirit we gain the power to overcome the world, the flesh and the devil. We receive new life and belong, once more, in the eternal family of our Father.

The Hebrew understanding is that each one, each *nephesh*, will stand before God in the flesh at the judgement to give their account, as described, for example, in Job 19:26-27 (KJV): "And though after my skin worms destroy this body, yet in my flesh shall I see God, whom I shall see for myself, and mine eyes shall behold, and not another, though my reins be consumed within me." 'Flesh' refers to a living body that is an individual human being. The Hebrew concept is of a unity made up of various parts, like the ear and the eye and the foot and the belly, and the mind and the heart and the soul and the spirit, that are interconnected and always belong together as a whole. As Paul says, when he compares the church to the physical body of a person, "The body is a unit, though it is made up of many parts; and though all its parts are many, they form one body …

The eye cannot say to the hand, "I don't need you!" And the head cannot say to the feet, "I don't need you!" On the contrary, those parts of the body that seem to be weaker are indispensable." (1 Corinthians 12:1 and 21-22.) Later in 1 Corinthians, in Chapter 15, Paul makes it clear that after we have passed through death we shall each be changed at our resurrection, so that then we each shall have an imperishable, spiritual body when we come to the Lord Jesus or stand before God.

If we allow ourselves to be changed in this world through the power of Holy Spirit working in our living bodies, we shall be able to give a better account, and we shall have a better resurrection (Hebrews 11:35, Matthew 15:14-30, Philippians 1:6, etc.). We need hearts that are humble enough to allow the Holy Spirit to do His work, here in this world, to change us and keep on changing us. The process actually continues throughout our lives. If we allow Him to do so, the Holy Spirit will make us aware of aspects of our lives, of the way we use our bodies, of the way we think, of the way we deal with our feelings, of the way we relate with other people, of the way we use things, and so on, that need to be reconciled to God in order to know His healing and peace concerning them.

Here is the way we claim inclusion in the victory Jesus won for us on the cross in an ongoing way: "Through the blood of Jesus I am redeemed out of the hand of the devil. Through the blood of Jesus all my sins are forgiven. Through the blood of Jesus I am continually being cleansed from all sin. Through the blood of Jesus I am justified, made righteous, just as if I'd never sinned. Through the blood of Jesus, I am sanctified, made holy, set apart to God. Through the blood of Jesus I have boldness to enter into the presence of God. The blood of Jesus cries out continually to God in heaven on my behalf."[167]

The application of the blood of our Lord Jesus must continue to be allowed to affect every part of our living being, every part of our hearts and minds and bodies. As we use words such as those, and as we really accept what Jesus did for us, that by His wounds we have been healed (1 Peter 2:24), it is necessary for us to allow connections, and associations, with the various parts of ourselves. Our hearts, or our minds, or our memories, or our emotions, or our behaviour, or some parts of our bodies, such as our bowels, or our lungs, or our skin, or our kidneys, may have been adversely affected by the fact that we have been living with particular aspects of our lives that were not properly reconciled to God.

The Hebrew way of talking about the various parts of the body in a way that is vital, giving obvious meaning to the function, will prove to be of very significant assistance for repentance and healing. In Hebrew the elements of words are known to root what is said in tactile truth, and the letters of written words are stylised pictures with basic meanings. For them language is the physical body speaking, and directly connecting with the world and with God.

Jesus says, "If your eye causes you to sin, pluck it out. It is better for you to enter the kingdom of God with one eye than to have two eyes and be thrown into hell, where their worm does not die and the fire is not

---

[167] These words are from Derek Prince.

quenched." (Mark 9:47-48, KJV.) This is tough language. It is clear that we should take drastic action when sin affects the body. Perhaps you think Jesus is over-stating His case. How can your eye cause you to sin? Well, it will be the functional organ most involved in that particular sin. Of course, the desire to sin with the eye originates in the heart; and therefore the heart will need to be made right with God, too, before the end organ is healed. Jesus was using a figure of speech to make a point.

You may argue that we live in the twenty-first century, and these days we know the heart is only a pump to pump the blood round the body, so how can we believe what Jesus, or what Jeremiah said? "In any case," you may say, "when Jeremiah says, "I the Lord search the heart and examine the mind to reward a man according to his conduct, according to what his deeds deserve" (Jeremiah 17:10), we do not any longer believe this applies to the physical heart!" "Well," I reply, "why not?" I vouch that more than forty years' experience as a physician has shown me that the relevant physical organs are indeed involved. And I believe that many other doctors might agree with me, were they not too frightened of the sanctions that would come against them for being politically incorrect if they were to say so.

I ask you now: "Do you believe your body is just a machine? Or is it part of your life? Is your mind the part of the machine that is in your brain? Does your actual physical heart respond to your thoughts? Where do your thoughts and desires come from? Are they just the product of biochemical reactions in your physiology? Does your heart actually miss a beat when you see the person you love after a long separation? Can love be accounted for through biochemistry? Are emotions just learned physiological responses to social events, or do they have more profound meaning and significance? Should they be allowed to affect our lives, or are our emotions to be suppressed and denied? Could spiritual influences affect our physiological functions?" There are many more such questions that could be asked. Why do so many people look to philosophers for the answers, instead of to the Holy Bible?

We can read in the Bible that the eye may be evil, desiring, unsatisfied, mocking, pitiless, proud. A concordance can easily provide the references. It is reasonable to believe these attributes could have some bearing on the development of disease in the eye. In fact experience proves this to be the case, although many people are reluctant to make the connection. The heart may be evil, wicked, hardened, closed, unyielding, craving, attached to others, enticed, stolen, adulterous, proud, despairing, bearing grudges, grieving, fearful, anguished, aching, resentful, passionate, cunning, wounded, broken, scornful, envious, anxious, faltering, disturbed, doubtful, dismayed, and so on. And it may also be sincere, peaceful, full of praise, joyful, wise, and prayerful. These qualities of the living heart may actually have a bearing upon physical heart disease. And such illness may be relieved when the heart is reconciled to God. There is very practical significance in the importance the Bible attaches to emotions and to being honest about them, feeling them, not hiding them, but rather reconciling them to God.

It is in the same sort of way that we read in the Bible that the bowels move in compassion, in mercy and in love. What woman does not know that her belly relaxes when breastfeeding her baby? Other emotions, too, may affect the functions of the belly. Distress and anger may be felt in the bowels, sometimes as a definite pain in the guts. In Chapter 4 at verse 19 Jeremiah says, "My bowels, my bowels! I am pained at my very heart; my heart maketh a noise in me..." Do we really believe that this has no bearing on what we call irritable bowel and gripe? We may be distressed, sometimes chronically distressed, when we do not know what to do with our feelings, and when we do not know what to do with what may seem to be our emotional waste matter – worries, disturbing memories, grief, confused emotions, stuff you cannot be bothered to think about or, perhaps, can never bear to think about. There is an association between this sort of thing and what we conceive of as our physical waste matter, excrement accumulated in the bowel until the bowels are opened and it is released. This sort of issue might have a bearing on illnesses of the bowels. And sometimes it might help to let it out and talk things through with someone you trust in order to clear the mind and the heart in order to bring the relevant issues to God in prayer in the name of the Lord Jesus. Sometimes this sort of thing takes time, and it is usually worthwhile to give time to it. The relief and the healing can be physical. In this sort of way we see how the mind and the emotions connect with the physical body and how diseases of the body might be healed.

In the same way a stiff neck may be related to obstinacy, and bone disease may be connected with envy or with some other cause of weakness of *ruach*, - see Proverbs 14:30: "A heart at peace gives life to the body, but envy rots the bones" and Proverbs 17:22: "A cheerful heart is good medicine, but a crushed spirit dries up the bones". And a sprained ankle may be connected no longer being sure on your feet due to loss of faith, or a curse, or not being alert to the enemy – see Deuteronomy 32:35, KJV: "…their foot shall slide in due time, for the day of their calamity is at hand, and the things that come upon them make haste." And liver disease may have some connection with grief (see Lamentations 2:11). And kidney disease may have some connection with an excess of restraint or, conversely, a foolish lack of it, for it seems that the Hebrews connected the kidneys with continence and, of course, with incontinence, as we may, too. The old Bible called the kidneys the reins. As reins enable a horse to be restrained and guided, so the kidneys were deemed to play a part in maintaining the consistency of one's very being in this world. Our very being rejoices amongst others who love us when we are moving in God's will: "Yea, my reins shall rejoice when thy lips speak right things." (Proverbs 23:16, KJV). And medical science shows the kidneys to be filters that retain necessary bio-chemicals whilst waste chemicals are excreted, which is a very necessary process for the chemical control of body fluids. In Hebrew thought physiology always has spiritual concomitants, and so it should in ours. Physic should never ignore metaphysics!

Metaphysics are especially relevant to the mind. Jesus heals disturbed minds and hearts, and the necessary spiritual knowledge should not be expected from secular psychiatric services that must cater for all belief systems.

Psychiatry takes twelve per cent of the National Health Service budget in the UK, more than any other discipline, and it is mainly concerned with controlling distress through medication, and removal of difficult people to places where they can be managed. Many people find the practice of psychiatry unsatisfactory. Even when people want real spiritual help, it is often effectively denied to them because Christian ministries often fail to understand the underlying problems. However, we find from the Bible that thoughts of the mind come and go, and minds may change, and the will may also change, according to the heart, and according to who is worshipped. If our heart be given to the Lord Jesus, whose love for us was so powerful that He overcame all the powers of the world, the flesh and the devil when He gave His life on a cross to redeem and save us, we too may overcome as He did. But although the demonised man who lived in the tombs of the Gerasenes was healed by Jesus very rapidly, for us these days healing may be a process that takes quite some time. And, if you think about it, the change after his healing would have affected all the relationships of that demonised man, which may well have been quite difficult for him.

The National Health Service is concerned with containment and care, but not, strictly speaking, with healing. Of course, some natural healing takes place all the time, by the grace of God; but Scripture ordains that it should be the business of the church to eradicate the spiritual roots of sickness and disease, so we need to make this much more available, particularly to those who seek the Lord Jesus for their healing. The Bible gives more clues for how this may be achieved than we have been accustomed to see. But it is necessary to read the Bible without a Greek bias.

Furthermore, it would be better if more Christians would accept that "If we claim to be without sin, we deceive ourselves and the truth is not in us." (1John 1:8.) It is time for the church to be inhospitable to hypocrites, such as Ananias and Sapphira in Acts 5, but hospitable to sinners. It is time for there to be more understanding of the human condition, more discerning of deception, of guilt, of the effects of betrayal, and of trauma. The best psychological textbook for it all is the Bible. I do not really believe we should need psychologists at all. I wish it were easier for Christians to confess their sins to each other and to pray for each other so that they may be healed (James 5:16). We should only confess to someone we trust, however, and it is time for many more Christians to be trustworthy.

One of the reasons we do not pray in depth with each other for healing is that people do not know what to do with what they learn of the lives of other people. They do not give what they hear, and what they feel about what they hear, and what it reminds them of, and all their own thoughts and feelings about it, to God. They do not put it all on the cross and say, "Thank you Lord Jesus." Sadly there are so very few mature Christians. We should never betray confidentiality and never, ever gossip. If we pray that the Lord will heal our tongues and give us self-control, He will; but He will also demand that we grow up in order properly to be able to use the self-control He gives us. Gossip and blackmail must be seen to have no place in Christian society.

Abstract dualistic Greek notions of soul as distinct from body, or of the immortality of the soul apart from the body, or the opposition of the soul to the body to explain moral evil, are foreign to Hebrew thought. So is any essential disconnection between the mind and the living body, or between the mind and the spirit. It is the whole person, with a body, that is accountable to God. It is the whole person, spirit, mind, soul and body that may be redeemed and saved through Jesus. And this salvation is an ongoing process that really happens in this world, in this life, in living bodies, including their sicknesses.

When all the books of the New Testament were written, difficulties arose in translating Hebrew concepts into Greek, which was then the prevailing language. And pagan and humanistic concepts, which were inevitably associated with Greek words, infiltrated the understanding of what was written, and distorted the true meaning. You can see some of the distortions: *Nephesh* became 'psyche', with all the associated ideas from the Greek philosopher Plato, who did not know the God of Israel. 'Psyche' has given us the word 'psychology', which has become the science of manipulating the mind, and 'psychiatry' which is supposed to be the medical discipline for healing the mind, although it does nothing of the sort. How withered *nephesh*, the concept of the soul, the very life of the body, has become for it to be translated 'mind'! And we also have the word 'psychic', which refers to people who listen to demons. 'Psyche' itself is sometimes translated 'soul', connoting the secular emotional and intellectual spirit of a person, divorced from the divine, and separate from the (mechanical) body. However, it is not all bad! You can actually use the English word 'soul' to begin to return to the Hebrew meaning of *nephesh* if you consider it to mean the living principle in a person. But it would be essential not to consider soul to be a separate entity. It is only the Holy Spirit that can make such divisions (Hebrews 4:12). And we should bear carefully in mind that many medical scientists actually dispute the existence of such an entity as the soul.

Ruach was translated into Greek as 'pneuma'. But in some ways the concept of 'spirit' was saved through being translated into the Latin as 'spiritus', which has been extensively used by the institutional church. Originally *ruach* meant 'breath', as well as 'spirit'. Although scientists do not involve themselves with the concept of spirit, many of them these days will take their astrology quite seriously, or indulge in other spiritual activities, such as Freemasonry, whilst denying that such things have any real significance! 'Pneuma' itself has only given us 'pneumonia', and one or two other 'pneuma' words like 'pneumatic'. Pneumonia does indeed seem more likely to afflict people who are dispirited, and it makes a person short of breath. In the English language spiritual influences and effects are conveyed in ways that seem to be either mundane or, conversely, unreal or otherworldly. The divine, sacred and holy are separated from everyday life. We are too secular to use the word 'spirit' in the way those Hebrews used *ruach*. Nevertheless, I am advocating that we rediscover Hebrew understanding and usage as fast as possible.

It is noteworthy that the Hebrew word for body, *geviyyah*, is very rare in the Hebrew Old Testament, being found only six times. Hebrews would more usually use the word for living flesh, *basar*, in order to refer specifically to the body. But when the Septuagint was written in Greek, in the third century BC, *basar* was often translated as 'soma', which was used fifty times. Unlike *basar*, 'soma' refers to the material body as opposed to the immaterial, that is, the part that receives life rather than has it. So with the Greek Septuagint there was already a weakening of the concept of *nephesh*, and a division between physical and spiritual, a duality causing lasting confusion. When, in English, we use the word 'somatic', that same duality is apparent. Our word 'somatic' describes the physical, mechanical body, as opposed to thoughts, feelings, emotions, intellect and living spirit.

For two thousand years it proved almost impossible to maintain true Hebrew understanding. But now, in these end times, God in His mercy has given the Jews their language again, and He is opening the ears and eyes and hearts of us Gentile Christians to get a grasp of the old biblical understanding. The whole idea that Greek and modern secular scientific thought and language have superseded the Hebrew by a process of some sort of godly evolution, and that it is therefore more appropriate and accurate, is nonsense. Indeed, the very idea that science shows us the truth is nonsense. Science reveals facts that are to be interpreted according to the truth of the word of God. The old Hebrew understanding of the nature of mankind, and of our relationships, and of our sicknesses, is utterly relevant right here and now.

When I meet someone, even if I meet them professionally as a physician, I do not want to be sceptically classifying them, like a classical Greek; I do not want to be seeing just the face they put on, or to be diagnosing them according to the clothes they are wearing or their medical history. Rather I want to begin to get to know the whole person beyond the parts, if they will allow me to do so, without prejudice, openly in the Lord.

However, meeting can often be a defensive game, because real true meeting may often seem rather threatening. People prefer to keep a lot hidden for fear of misunderstanding or rejection, or worse. They often try to defend themselves by hiding behind various disguises, stereotyping and personal prejudices. Sometimes it can seem very convenient to have a diagnosis to excuse oneself. If honest business is to be done, however, there comes a point when sufficient common understanding is necessary. We cannot trust another person unless we know them sufficiently. Authentic meeting and honest business can only truly occur in the name of the Lord Jesus. Let us be glad that the Holy Spirit gives discernment.

But if someone believes they are sick or crazy, who am I to judge them? If they want me to be their physician I shall try to determine with them what might be amiss, and try to find a way to healing for the whole person. But I shall require that they agree not to objectify their bodies or their minds as if they were machines, and to endeavour to give godly meaning to everything that has happened and is happening, including their thoughts and their memories and their emotions and their sicknesses and behaviour. And they would have to do away with the stiff upper lip and to stop trying to be strong. And they would have to agree that truth is not an abstraction, but a person with whom to have a relationship.

I have not prescribed drugs for many years – I leave it to others, to do that if it really seems necessary. People often do not need medication, and will often find healing if they connect what is going on in their bodies with godly meaning, and then find reconciliation with God through Jesus.

Although I am a medical doctor, I reckon many people in churches should be doing the sort of work I have been doing. For two thousand years doctors have been doing a job that really belongs to Christian deacons.

Furthermore, the Christian theological doctrine of mankind needs to be adequate to the truth of all human experience, not just experience that lies safely outside scientific medical and psychological classifications of disease and abnormality, which are essentially Greek. My theology, furthermore, is Arminian, and I believe no one to be beyond redemption.

Look! Jesus redeems the whole *nephesh* (spirit, soul and body) so that our bodies might be temples of the Holy Spirit, and be presented to God as living sacrifices. 1 Corinthians 6:19-20 says, "Do you not know that your body is a temple of the Holy Spirit, who is in you, whom you have received from God? You are not your own; you were bought at a price. Therefore honour God with your body." And Romans 12:1-2 says, "Therefore I urge you, brothers, in view of God's mercy, to offer your bodies as living sacrifices, holy and pleasing to God – this is your spiritual act of worship. Do not conform any longer to the pattern of this world…"

Holy Spirit dissolves dividing walls of dissociation, and enables us to make connections with previously hidden aspects of ourselves, and develop godly understanding that is not of this world (1 Corinthians 1:18 – 2:16). All things hold together in Him to whom we must give account. Holy Spirit brings matters to light, concerning both our personal lives and the world around us. We are to bring it all before Him and lay it on the cross of the Lord Jesus so that He may change us and heal us with His resurrection power, in order the His presence in the world may be reflected more fully in our lives.

So here is a prayer for commitment:

"Almighty God, Creator of the universe, thank you for your love and your mercy and for sending your only begotten son, the Lord Jesus Christ of Nazareth, to save people so we may belong with you in your kingdom and call you Father. I know Jesus' blood was shed for me. I know he was crucified on a cross and died for my sin, and was buried but rose from the dead the third day. He overcame all the powers of death and Satan. He redeemed me and made atonement for me with his blood. With all my heart I confess my sin and accept what he has done for me. Thank you for saving me. From now on Jesus Christ is my king, and he reigns in my heart. Thank you for sending Holy Spirit so that I may know you and understand your words and overcome the world, the flesh and the devil like Jesus did. Please continue to change me and heal me and equip me for eternal life with you."

Other titles from John Gordon

Healing for the Wounded Life – How to understand
your illness and find biblical solutions

**Healing the Divided Self – Freedom from states of
mind and mental illness**

Schizophrenia - A Christian understanding

www.philadelphiabooks.co.uk

Lightning Source UK Ltd.
Milton Keynes UK
UKOW06f1033190615

253788UK00006B/99/P